KU-002-178

CONTEMPORARY AMERICAN ARCHITECTS

KU-002-178

CONTEMPORARY
AMERICAN ARCHITECTS

BY PHILIP JODIDIO

TASCHEN
KÖLN LISBOA LONDON NEW YORK OSAKA PARIS

Frontispiece · Frontispiz · Frontispice
Helmut Jahn: Northwestern Terminal, Chicago, Illinois, 1979-86
© Photo: Timothy Hursley

Page 6 · Seite 6 · Page 6
Robert Venturi: Gordon Wu Hall, Princeton University, New Jersey, 1980-83
© Photo: Paul Warchol

**This book was printed on 100% chlorine-free bleached
paper in accordance with the TCF-standard**

© 1993 Benedikt Taschen Verlag GmbH
Hohenzollernring 53, D-50672 Köln

By Philip Jodidio, Paris
Designed and text edited by Barbro Garenfeld Büning, Cologne
Cover design: Angelika Muthesius, Cologne; Mark Thomson, London
German translation: Franca Fritz, Heinrich Koop, Cologne
French translation: Jacques Bosser, Paris

Printed in Italy
ISBN 3-8228-9454-0

CONTENTS

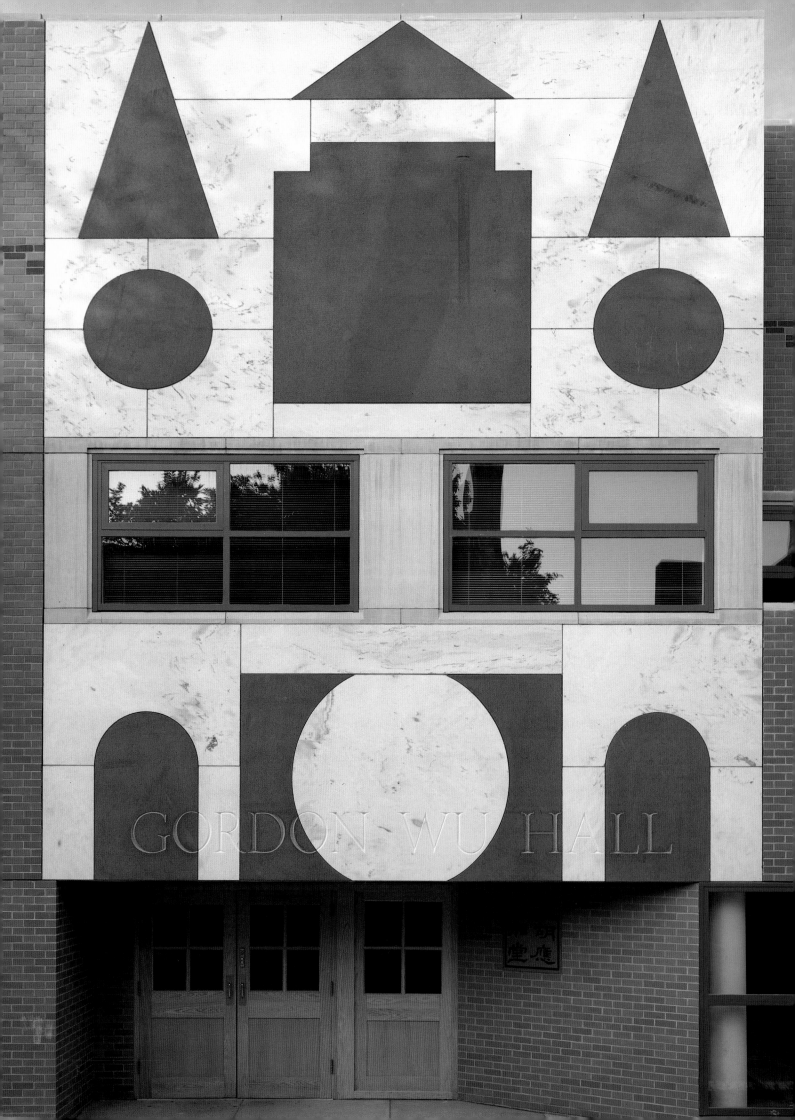

GORDON WU HALL

CONTEMPORARY
AMERICAN ARCHITECTS

BY PHILIP JODIDIO

TASCHEN

KÖLN LISBOA LONDON NEW YORK OSAKA PARIS

Frontispiece · Frontispiz · Frontispice
Helmut Jahn: Northwestern Terminal, Chicago, Illinois, 1979-86
© Photo: Timothy Hursley

Page 6 · Seite 6 · Page 6
Robert Venturi: Gordon Wu Hall, Princeton University, New Jersey, 1980-83
© Photo: Paul Warchol

**This book was printed on 100% chlorine-free bleached
paper in accordance with the TCF-standard**

© 1993 Benedikt Taschen Verlag GmbH
Hohenzollernring 53, D-50672 Köln

By Philip Jodidio, Paris
Designed and text edited by Barbro Garenfeld Büning, Cologne
Cover design: Angelika Muthesius, Cologne; Mark Thomson, London
German translation: Franca Fritz, Heinrich Koop, Cologne
French translation: Jacques Bosser, Paris

Printed in Italy
ISBN 3-8228-9454-0

AMERICAN ARCHITECTURE TODAY
AMERIKANISCHE ARCHITEKTUR HEUTE
L'ARCHITECTURE AMERICAINE CONTEMPORAINE
by Philip **Jodidio**

Contemporary American architects often make reference to local tradition in their work, as though the United States could call on a history as rich and varied as that of Europe, which of course it cannot. To this day, American architecture, like the very history of the country, is the product of a wide range of influences, the most important of which clearly found their origin in the »old« continent.

Louis Mumford in his work »Roots of Contemporary American Architecture« (1952), points out that even the log cabin, which might seem to be the epitome of native invention, was in fact a form of construction brought by the Swedes to Delaware in the 18th century. Especially before the end of the 19th century, architecture in America was forcibly the expression, however, of the ambitions, and of the life-style imposed by the New World on the successive waves of immigrants and such did begin to evolve in some instances away from European models quite early, especially when more ephemeral, lighter types of architecture were involved. Although stately stone buildings appeared quite early in the cities of the East Coast, for example, these were largely, as might be the case in Boston, or Philadelphia for example, variants of the Georgian style, launched in England as Palladianism by Lord Burlington, or elegant Neo-Classical edifices like Charles Bulfinch's State House (Boston, MA, 1795-98) which is based on Somerset House in London.

Zeitgenössische amerikanische Architekten greifen in ihren Arbeiten häufig auf traditionelle Einflüsse ihrer Heimat zurück, als hätten die Vereinigten Staaten eine ähnlich reiche Geschichte wie Europa, was natürlich nicht stimmt. Dabei ist die amerikanische Architektur – wie das Land selbst – bis zum heutigen Tage das Produkt einer Vielzahl von Strömungen, von denen die wichtigsten ihren Ursprung ganz offensichtlich in der »alten« Welt haben.

In seinem Buch »Roots of Contemporary American Architecture« (1952) legt Louis Mumford dar, daß selbst das Blockhaus als Inbegriff uramerikanischer Erfindungsgabe in Wahrheit während des 18. Jahrhunderts von den Schweden nach Delaware gebracht wurde. Vor allem in der Zeit vor der Jahrhundertwende spiegelte die amerikanische Architektur zwangsläufig die Ambitionen und den Lebensstil der Einwandererwellen, denen die Neue Welt ausgesetzt war. Dies gilt vor allem für vorläufigere und leichtere Bauweisen.

In den Städten der Ostküste entstanden bereits relativ früh die ersten imposanten Steinhäuser. Dabei handelte es sich, wie beispielsweise in Boston, größtenteils um Variationen des Georgian Style, in England durch Lord Burlington auch als Palladianismus bekanntgeworden, oder um klassizistische Gebäude wie das von Charles Bulfinch erbaute State House (Boston, Massachusetts, 1795-98), dessen Architektur auf dem Somerset House in London basiert.

Les architectes américains contemporains font souvent référence dans leur travail à la tradition locale, comme si leur pays pouvait s'appuyer sur une histoire aussi riche que celle de l'Europe. Comme l'histoire des Etats-Unis, celle de l'architecture américaine est en fait à ce jour le produit de multiples influences dont les plus importantes trouvent à l'évidence leur origine sur le «vieux» continent.

Louis Mumford, dans son livre «Roots of Contemporary American Architecture» (1952) souligne que même la cabane de rondins, qui peut apparaître comme l'expression par excellence de l'inventivité locale, fut en réalité introduite au Delaware par des Suédois au XVIIIème siècle. En Amérique, et tout particulièrement jusqu'à la fin du XIXème siècle, l'architecture fut par force et d'une manière ou d'une autre l'expression des ambitions et d'un style de vie imposé par le Nouveau Monde à ses vagues successives d'immigrants. Dans certain cas, elle s'éloigne vite des modèles européens. Même si de nobles demeures de pierre ont fait assez tôt leur apparition dans les villes de la côte Est, comme à Boston par exemple, elles furent essentiellement des variantes du style géorgien, lancé en Angleterre sous le nom de palladianisme par Lord Burlington, ou des édifices néo-classiques, ainsi qu'en témoigne la Résidence du Gouverneur de Charles Bulfinch (Boston, Massachusetts, 1795-98) inspirée de Somerset House à Londres.

Thomas Jefferson: Monticello, Charlottesville, Virginia, 1769-1825

Defining American Architecture

Thomas Jefferson's famous Monticello (Charlottesville, VA, 1769-1825), cited as an example of Colonial accomplishment, is clearly an expression, at least in its definitive form, of the »Greek Revival« phase of European Neoclassicism. It bears more than a passing resemblance to Chiswick House, begun near London by Lord Burlington and William Kent in 1725, which in turn was inspired by the Villa Rotonda (Andrea Palladio, Vicenza, c. 1567-70). The names of other American styles which followed the Greek Revival; the Egyptian, Gothic and Romanesque Revivals, or the Italian Villa Style, indicate by their very names a lack of originality. Buildings like Monticello retain an elegance which was to characterise many subsequent American buildings, but other types of construction might be considered more innovative.

Such might be the case for the wooden frame-houses first built on the East Coast in the late 17th century, but in most instances, European influences can be readily determined, despite the adaptation to local circumstances. Thus the Boardman House (Saugus, MA, 1686), a two-story structure with a central chimney, is directly related to 17th century English equivalents. The Dyckman House (New York, NY, 1783) shows its Dutch Colonial origins, just as the J. B. Valle House (Ste. Genevieve, MI, c. 1800) is a testimony to the influence of

Definitionen amerikanischer Architektur

Thomas Jeffersons berühmtes Monticello (Charlottesville, Virginia, 1769-1825), das als vollendetes Beispiel des Kolonialstils gilt, ist zumindest aufgrund seiner klar umrissenen Form Ausdruck des europäischen Neoklassizismus, der den griechischen Stil wiederentdeckte. Dieses Bauwerk weist mehr als nur eine oberflächliche Ähnlichkeit mit Chiswick House auf, dessen Bau Lord Burlington und William Kent im Jahr 1725 in der Nähe von London begannen und für das seinerseits die Villa Rotonda (Andrea Palladio, Vicenza, ca. 1567-70) Pate gestanden hatte. Die der Wiederbelebung des griechischen Stils folgenden Richtungen wie etwa das Ägyptische, die Gotik, die Romanik sowie der Italienische Landhausstil lassen bereits aufgrund ihrer Namen auf einen gewissen Mangel an Originalität schließen. Obwohl solche Bauwerke wie das Monti-

Définir l'architecture américaine

Le célèbre Monticello de Thomas Jefferson (Charlottesville, Virginie, 1769-1825) cité comme exemple de réussite du style colonial est l'expression, du moins dans sa forme définitive, de la phase du retour à l'antique du néo-classicisme européen. Elle révèle plus qu'une ressemblance avec Chiswick House, construite à partir de 1725 par Lord Burlington et William Kent à Londres et inspirée par la Villa Rotonda d'Andrea Palladio (Vicence, vers 1567-70). Les styles américains qui succédèrent à ce retour à l'antique, l'égyptien, le gothique, et le roman, ou le style villa italienne, trahissent par leur nom même leur manque d'originalité. Si Monticello annonce l'élégance qui allait caractériser de nombreux bâtiments américains ultérieurs, d'autres types de construction peuvent néanmoins être considérés comme plus innovateurs.

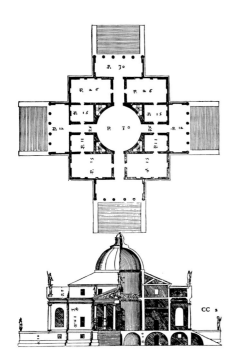

the French. Whatever European influences they evolved from, some large, late 18th century wooden houses, like that of John Brown, on College Hill in Providence, Rhode Island, do show an elegance and architectural ambition of which present day historical preservationists are justifiably proud. In other areas, such as the Southwest, more original solutions evolved as a result of local conditions, as in the case of the San Estevan church built by Franciscans in Acoma, New Mexico of adobe and fieldstone between 1629 and 1644. The significance of adobe architecture, which certainly predated the arrival of the Spaniards, remains evident to this day through the work of designers like Antoine Predock.

cello eine Eleganz aufweisen, die Charakteristikum zahlreicher späterer amerikanischer Gebäude wurde, könnte man andere Konstruktionsweisen eher als innovativ bezeichnen.

Dies gilt beispielsweise für die Holzhäuser an der Ostküste, die dort gegen Ende des 17. Jahrhunderts entstanden. Aber in den meisten Fällen lassen sich, trotz Anpassung an die jeweilige Situation vor Ort, die europäischen Wurzeln leicht nachweisen. So auch beim Boardman House (Saugus, Massachusetts, 1686), einem zweistöckigen Gebäude mit zentralem Kamin, das sich direkt an englischen Vorbildern des 17. Jahrhunderts orientiert. Das Dyckman House (New York, 1783) zeigt deutlich seine von niederländischen Siedlern geprägte Herkunft, während das J. B. Valle House (Ste. Genevieve, Michigan, ca. 1800) den französischen Einfluß dokumentiert. Welchem europäischen Hintergrund sie ihre Entstehung auch immer verdanken, die großen Holzhäuser des späten 18. Jahrhunderts - wie das Haus von John Brown auf dem College Hill in Providence, Rhode Island – zeugen von einer Eleganz und einem architektonischen Anspruch, auf die heutige Denkmalpfleger zu Recht stolz sind. In anderen Gegenden, etwa im Südwesten, fand man eigenständige Lösungen für die jeweiligen örtlichen Gegebenheiten. Als frühes Beispiel für diesen Baustil gilt die San Estevan Kirche, die zwischen 1629 und 1644 in Acoma, Neu-Mexiko von Franziskanern aus Lehmzie-

Tel pourrait être le cas des maisons à structure de bois construites sur la côte Est à partir de la fin du XVIIème siècle, même si, dans la plupart des cas, des influences européennes peuvent être rapidement identifiées quels que soient les efforts d'adaptation aux circonstances locales. Ainsi la Boardman House (Saugus, Massachusetts, 1686), structure de deux étages à cheminée centrale, rappelle-t-elle fortement ses équivalents anglais du XVIIème siècle. La Dyckman House (New York, NY, 1783) affiche ses origines néerlandaises coloniales, de même que la J. B. Valle House (Ste. Genevieve, Michigan, vers 1800) illustre l'influence française. Quelle que soit l'origine européenne de leur inspiration, certaines grandes demeures à structure de bois de la fin du XVIIIème siècle, comme celle de John Brown, à College Hill (Providence, Rhode Island), affirment une élégance et une ambition architecturale dont les défenseurs actuels du patrimoine peuvent être fiers à juste titre. Dans d'autres régions, comme le Sud-Ouest, des solutions plus originales se firent jour pour répondre à la spécificité des conditions locales, comme dans le cas de l'église San Estevan construite par les Franciscains à Acoma (Nouveau-Mexique) en adobe et en pierre des champs (1629-44). L'importance de l'architecture d'adobe, certainement antérieure à l'arrivée des Espagnols, reste encore évidente aujourd'hui dans les travaux de créateurs comme Antoine Predock.

Antoine Predock: Hotel Santa Fe, Euro
Disney, Marne-la-Vallée, France, 1992

Perhaps more interesting, in terms of
the fundamental originality of more recent American architecture, and even
for its potential contribution to future
creativity, is the transient life imposed
by the conquest of the West. The dream
of endless spaces, of a nature whose
spiritual quality was best expressed by
painters of the Hudson River School, or
by the German Albert Bierstadt, is
somehow deeply inscribed in the char-
acter of the United States, where an ex-
ceedingly large proportion of the population by European standards, thinks
nothing, even today, of simply moving
on to another city or state in the hope of
finding a better life.

When the shores of the Pacific were
reached, the desire to keep moving remained, and recently a more sterile culture emerged, based on the auto-

geln und Feldsteinen errichtet wurde.
Die Bedeutung des Lehmziegelbaus,
der sich mit Sicherheit schon vor die
Zeit der spanischen Kolonialherrschaft
zurückdatieren läßt, ist bis heute in den
Werken von Designern wie Antoine Predock erhalten geblieben.

Bezüglich der fundamentalen Eigenständigkeit der jüngeren amerikanischen Architektur und ihres potentiellen
Anteils an künftigen Werken, ist die un-
beständige Lebensweise, die die Erobe-
rung des Westens mit sich brachte,
wahrscheinlich viel interessanter. Der
Traum von endloser Weite, von einer
Natur, deren Geist die Künstler der Hudson River School oder der Deutsch-
Amerikaner Albert Bierstadt am ein-
dringlichsten wiedergegeben haben,
dieser Traum ist tief im Charakter der
Vereinigten Staaten verwurzelt. Ein ste-

Peut-être plus intéressant encore, en terme d'originalité fondamentale d'une architecture américaine plus récente, et
même pour sa contribution potentielle à
une créativité à venir, est la vie inconstan-
te issue de la conquête de l'Ouest. Le
rêve d'espaces infinis et d'une nature
dont la qualité spirituelle fut merveilleu-
sement exprimée par les peintres de
l'«Hudson River School» ou par l'Allemand Albert Bierstadt, est d'une certaine
façon profondément inscrit dans le caractère des Etats-Unis. Encore aujourd'hui,
une très large proportion de la population,
par rapport aux critères européens, n'at-
tache aucune importance particulière à
changer de ville ou d'Etat dans l'espoir
d'y trouver une vie meilleure.

Lorsque les côtes du Pacifique furent at-
teintes, ce désir de mouvement persista,
et apparut une forme de culture plus

mobiles and mobile homes that continue to ply the highways of America. From the wagon trains rendered familiar by Westerns, to the architectural forms fashioned from available materials, principally wood, it might be said that necessity drove Americans to differentiate themselves from their European ancestors. Enormous spaces had to be covered, cities built and rebuilt in a very short lapse of time. A light, or even ephemeral type of architecture was best adopted to the change and movement which are as deeply rooted in the history of the United States as are tradition and a certain immobility in Europe.

American Styles and Contemporary Trends

In his essential book »Complexity and Contradiction in Architecture« (1966), Robert Venturi compares Las Vegas and Los Angeles to Florence and Rome. The whimsical, blustery symbols of transience and superficiality are thus likened to the most profound and lasting creations of European intelligence. In fact, American architecture, when it is merely an imitation of European tradition is usually quite bad. It is much better when it accepts that the real sources and common ground available to American builders are in the hybrid culture of the United States, where Mickey Mouse has as much relevance as Brunelleschi. In a less negative way, it can be said that there are two basic lines of creativity; one is an urge to break rules and conquer

tig wachsender Teil der Bevölkerung findet selbst heute nichts dabei, einfach in eine andere Stadt oder einen anderen Staat zu ziehen, immer in der Hoffnung auf ein besseres Leben.

Als die Küste des pazifischen Ozeans erreicht war, blieb das Verlangen nach Mobilität bestehen. In der jüngeren Vergangenheit entstand eine etwas sterilere Kultur, die auf Automobilen oder sogar Mobilheimen basiert, die unaufhörlich die endlosen amerikanischen Highways auf und ab fahren. Reine Notwendigkeit zwang die Amerikaner, sich von ihren europäischen Vorfahren abzugrenzen. Und diese Entwicklung reicht von den aus zahlreichen Western wohlbekannten Planwagen bis hin zu Architekturformen, die sich den verfügbaren Materialien – hauptsächlich Holz – anpaßten. Innerhalb kurzer Zeit mußten große Flächen erschlossen, Städte gebaut und wieder neu aufgebaut werden. Eine leichte oder sogar kurzlebige Architektur wurde dem Bedürfnis nach Veränderung und Wechsel am ehesten gerecht, ein Bedürfnis, das in der Geschichte der Vereinigten Staaten so tief verwurzelt ist wie in Europa traditionelle Werte und eine gewisse Immobilität.

Amerikanische Stilrichtungen und heutige Trends

In seinem grundlegenden Buch »Complexity and Contradiction in Architecture« (1966, dt. 1978) vergleicht Robert Venturi Las Vegas und Los Angeles mit Florenz und Rom. Die launenhaften,

stérile fondée sur l'automobile ou les «mobile homes», qui continue à marquer les routes de l'Amérique. Depuis les convois de chariots popularisés par les westerns jusqu'aux formes architecturales liées à la disponibilité des matériaux, le bois principalement, on peut dire que la nécessité poussa les Américains à se différencier de leurs ancêtres européens. De vastes espaces devaient être conquis, des cités construites et reconstruites dans des délais très courts et un type d'architecture légère, ou même éphémère, fut adopté pour répondre à ces changements et à ce mouvement perpétuels qui sont autant enracinés dans l'histoire des Etats-Unis que l'authenticité des traditions et une certaine sédentarité le sont en Europe.

Styles américains et tendances contemporaines

Dans son ouvrage essentiel «Complexity and Contradiction in Architecture» (1966), Robert Venturi compare Las Vegas et Los Angeles à Florence et Rome. Les symboles bizarres et voyants de la précarité et de la superficialité sont ainsi rapprochés des créations les plus nobles et les plus intemporelles de l'esprit européen. En fait, l'architecture américaine est d'habitude assez médiocre lorsqu'elle se contente d'imiter les traditions européennes. Elle est d'une qualité bien meilleure lorsqu'elle admet que ses vraies sources et son terreau commun ont pour origine une culture hybride où Mickey Mouse a autant de perti-

new territories, and the other is the desire to build solidly and well without concern for extreme originality.

The first of these categories shares a sense of challenge, excitement and movement, much akin to the qualities

engendered by the conquest of the great expanses of the West. The generation of American architects who currently have the most influence, men like Frank Gehry, have seized on forms and materials which sometimes project an impression of chaotic disorder, or inherent transience. Gehry takes materials which might be at hand, like corrugated metal or chain-link fence, and integrates them into structures, where most critics

prahlerischen Symbole von Vergänglichkeit und Oberflächlichkeit werden also den größten und zeitlosesten Kunstwerken europäischen Geistes gegenübergestellt. Tatsächlich ist die amerikanische Architektur im allgemeinen ziemlich schlecht, so lange es sich nur um reine Nachahmung europäischer Traditionen handelt. Sie ist erheblich besser und origineller, sobald die amerikanischen Architekten akzeptieren, daß ihre wahren Quellen und Ursprünge in der Mischkultur der Vereinigten Staaten liegen, in der Mickey Mouse den gleichen Status besitzt wie Brunelleschi. Weniger negativ formuliert läßt sich feststellen, daß es zwei Grundformen von Kreativität gibt: zum einen den Drang, sich über alle Regeln hinwegzusetzen und neue Gebiete zu erobern, und zum anderen das Bemühen, solide und beständig zu bauen, ohne dabei übermäßig großen Wert auf Originalität zu legen.

Die erste dieser beiden Kategorien zeichnet sich durch ein Element der Herausforderung, Spannung und Bewegung aus, das auch in den großen Eroberungen des Westens zum Ausdruck kommt. Die Generation amerikanischer Architekten mit dem größten Einfluß auf die heutige Zeit – wie Frank Gehry – haben auf Formen und Materialien zurückgegriffen, die teilweise den Eindruck chaotischer Unordnung oder Flüchtigkeit erwecken. Gehry verwendet scheinbar zufällig vorhandene Materialien wie Wellblech oder Maschendraht

nence que Brunelleschi. D'une façon moins négative, on peut dire qu'il existe deux grandes lignes de créativité, l'une correspond à un besoin de briser les règles et de conquérir de nouveaux territoires, l'autre à celui de construire bien et solidement, sans se soucier d'une originalité excessive.

La première de ces catégories traduit un sens du défi, de la surexcitation et du mouvement très apparenté aux qualités engendrées par la conquête des grands espaces de l'Ouest. Toute une génération d'architectes américains, ceux qui exercent actuellement le plus d'influence tel Frank Gehry, se sont emparés de formes et de matériaux qui parfois projettent une impression de désordre chaotique, ou d'inconstance intrinsèque. Gehry utilise les matériaux facilement disponibles comme la tôle ondulée ou le treillis de fil-de-fer et les intègre dans des structures où la plupart des critiques sont bien en peine de trouver des symboles de permanence et de solidité. Bien qu'ils ne soient pas nécessairement éphémères, ses bâtiments projettent un sens du mouvement qui peut être considéré comme typiquement américain.

Né à Chicago, le gratte-ciel est l'un des meilleurs symboles de l'audace grandissante de la bonne architecture américaine. Pris individuellement, ces tours ne semblent guère pouvoir prétendre à la spiritualité des grandes œuvres de l'architecture européenne et cependant, d'une certaine façon, l'accumulation de

will be looking for symbols of permanence and solidity. Although not necessarily ephemeral, his buildings project a sense of movement which might be called typically American.

The skyscraper, born in Chicago, is as good a symbol as any of the upward reaching audacity of good American architecture. Individually, skyscrapers would seem to make very little claim to the sort of spirituality implicit in the great buildings of Europe, and yet somehow, the accumulation of spires that forms Manhattan projects a sense of human achievement and potential that the old continent only rarely attains today.

The very idea of searching for typically American characteristics in architecture, though, is undoubtedly illusory. As was emphasized above, the very nature of

und verarbeitet sie zu Strukturen, bei denen die meisten Kritiker nach Symbolen für Beständigkeit und Festigkeit suchen. Obwohl seine Bauwerke nicht unbedingt kurzlebig sind, spiegeln sie ein Gefühl von Bewegung, das man typisch amerikanisch nennen könnte.

Der Wolkenkratzer, dessen Geburtsstätte in Chicago lag, ist ein klassisches Symbol für die aufwärtsstrebende Kühnheit guter amerikanischer Architektur. Obwohl ein einzelnes dieser Gebäude nur wenig von der Geisteshaltung erkennen läßt, die den großen Bauwerken Europas zu eigen ist, vermittelt die Ansammlung von Spitzen, die Manhattan bildet, ein Gefühl für menschliche Errungenschaften und Möglichkeiten, das die alte Welt heute nur selten aufweist.

Dennoch ist die Suche nach typisch amerikanischen Eigenschaften in der Architektur unzweifelhaft illusorisch. Wie bereits erwähnt, läßt schon die Vielschichtigkeit der Vereinigten Staaten den Schluß zu, daß auch ihre Architektur die Summe vieler verschiedener Einzelteile ist. Die heutige Zeit kennt keine dominierende Stilrichtung, so daß Architekten ebenso legitim zeitgenössische Formen der Moderne vertreten wie auch nach neuen und aufregenden Formen suchen können. Die Gebäude eines I. M. Pei etwa verliehen vielen sehr unterschiedlichen Städten wie Hongkong (Bank of China Tower), Paris (Pyramide im Louvre) und Washington (National Gallery's East Building) neue

flèches qui forme Manhattan projette un sens de l'accomplissement et des potentialités de l'homme que le vieux monde semble rarement en mesure d'atteindre de nos jours.

L'idée même de rechercher des caractéristiques typiquement américaines dans l'architecture de ce pays est cependant sans aucun doute illusoire. Comme il a été montré plus haut, la nature même des Etats-Unis implique que son architecture soit la somme de ses différentes composantes. Aujourd'hui, en l'absence de style dominant, les architectes qui défendent les versions contemporaines du Modernisme sont aussi légitimes dans leur action que ceux qui explorent de nouvelles formes plus surprenantes. Les immeubles de I. M. Pei, par exemple, qui constituent autant de nouveaux symboles pour des cités aussi différentes que Hong Kong (Tour de la Banque de Chine), Paris (la Pyramide du Louvre) et Washington (Bâtiment Est de la National Gallery), ne participent pas à cette course aux gadgets visuels et à l'émotion bon marché qui inspira tant Robert Venturi à Las Vegas. Ils aspirent à une permanence qui doit sans doute autant à la Chine natale de Pei qu'aux racines européennes du Modernisme.

Après une période (la fin des années 70, début des années 80) consacrée à l'invocation des fantômes de la tradition sous la forme pastiche du post-modernisme, l'architecture américaine dans son ensemble s'est orientée selon deux grandes tendances. L'une, représentée dans

the United States already implies that its architecture will be the sum of many different parts. Today, with no dominant style, the architects who defend contemporary versions of Modernism are as legitimate as those who are seeking startling new forms. The buildings of I. M. Pei, for example, which have given new symbols to cities as different as Hong Kong (Bank of China Tower), Paris (the Louvre Pyramid) and Washington (the National Gallery's East Building) do not share the gadgety search for the cheap thrill that so inspired Robert Venturi in Las Vegas. They aspire to a permanence that may have as much to do

Wahrzeichen, ohne dabei der hartnäckigen Suche nach billigen Reizen zu verfallen, die Robert Venturi in Las Vegas so inspirierten. Sie streben nach einer Beständigkeit, die sich zu gleichen Teilen aus Peis chinesischer Herkunft wie auch aus den europäischen Wurzeln der Moderne erklären läßt.

Nach einer Periode des postmodernen Mischmaschs, bei der gegen Ende der siebziger und Anfang der achtziger Jahre die Geister der Tradition beschworen wurden, kristallisierten sich in der amerikanischen Architektur zwei größere Strömungen heraus. Eine Richtung – hier vertreten durch Gehry, Eisenman,

ce livre par Gehry, Eisenman, Eric Owen Moss ou Morphosis, s'efforce de briser les formes standardisées du Modernisme et de rechercher d'autres paradigmes. La comparaison avec les travaux des pionniers constructivistes russes semble inévitable, sauf qu'à la différence de ceux-ci, les Américains ont, eux, vraiment les moyens d'édifier le nouveau monde qu'ils imaginent. Dans le sillage intellectuel de Gehry, des architectes plus jeunes, comme Eric Owen Moss, ont commencé à prendre en compte les attentes de base qui existent autour des rapports entre l'environnement et le construit. On trouve dans son œuvre des

William van Alen: Chrysler Building, New York, New York, 1927-30

with Pei's native China as with the European roots of Modernism.

After a period, in the late 1970's and early 1980's, of calling up the ghosts of tradition in the form of the Post-Modern pastiche, American architecture as a whole has moved on to two larger trends. One, represented in this book by Gehry, Eisenman, Eric Owen Moss or Morphosis, seeks to break up standard Modernist forms and to search for other paradigms. The comparison to the pion-

Eric Owen Moss und Morphosis – bricht bewußt mit den Standardformen der Moderne und sucht nach neuen Ausdrucksmöglichkeiten. Der Vergleich mit den Pionierarbeiten der russischen Konstruktivisten scheint unvermeidlich, aber im Gegensatz zu ihnen haben die Amerikaner auch die Mittel und Möglichkeiten, ihre neue Welt zu verwirklichen. Unter Gehrys intellektueller Führung begannen junge Architekten wie Eric Owen Moss damit, gegen die grundlegenden Erwartungen an eine architektonische Wirklichkeit anzugehen. Die Verwendung exzentrischer Formen und Materialien in Moss' Arbeiten hat häufig einen provokativen oder sogar aggressiven Beigeschmack. Wie in vielen Werken der zeitgenössischen Kunst herrscht auch hier der Grundgedanke, daß traditionelle ästhetische Werte wie Schönheit und/oder Harmonie entschieden abgelehnt werden müssen. Andere, wie Helmut Jahn und Arquitectonica, haben eigene, neue Wege gefunden, das moderne Vokabular einzusetzen. Neben verschiedenen technischen Neuerungen ermöglicht diesen Architekten auch ihr eigenes Selbstverständnis einen großen Abstand zu den Doktrinen der Moderne, die ihrerseits den politischen Idealen des Bauhaus entstammten. Mit einem seiner neuesten Gebäude stimmte Helmut Jahn, der in Nürnberg geborene und in den Vereinigten Staaten populär gewordene Architekt, bei seiner Rückkehr nach Deutschland keinen Lob-,

formes et des matériaux excentriques qui souvent jouent de la provocation ou même de la violence. On voit ici à l'œuvre, comme dans une bonne part de l'art contemporain, une notion qui veut que les considérations esthétiques classiques sur la beauté et/ou l'harmonie doivent être rejetées avec force. D'autres, comme Helmut Jahn, ou Arquitectonica, ont choisi d'utiliser le vocabulaire moderniste d'une manière nouvelle. La maturité de ces architectes, de même que certaines avancées techniques, leur permet de se distancier encore davantage d'une forme de modernisme doctrinaire née de l'idéologie du Bauhaus. A l'occasion d'une de ses œuvres récentes, Helmut Jahn, né à Nuremberg mais ayant fait carrière aux Etats-Unis, est revenu en Allemagne non pour rendre hommage à la géométrie anonyme de l'architecture Bauhaus mais plutôt pour l'enterrer. Sa tour de la Foire de Francfort (1992), rejette le dessin rectiligne de tant de tours modernes pour prendre des formes clairement évocatrices des gratte-ciel Art-Déco new-yorkais de la fin des années 20 et du début des années 30. Ce glissement transatlantique de formes et d'influences montre que même si beaucoup des idées architecturales originales du XXème siècle sont venues d'Europe, elles ont pris leur forme définitive et doivent leur acceptation aux Etats-Unis. Même si Walter Gropius ou Ludwig Mies van der Rohe enseignèrent aux Etats-Unis et y exercèrent une énorme influence, leurs théories socialistes n'y prirent

16

sondern einen Schwanengesang auf die anonyme Geometrie der Bauhaus-Architektur an. Sein Frankfurter Messeturm (1992) entspricht nicht dem geradlinigen Design vieler moderner Wolkenkratzer, sondern weist eine eigenständige Form auf, die an die New Yorker Art deco-Türme der späten zwanziger und frühen dreißiger Jahre erinnert.

Diese transatlantische Verschiebung von Formen und Einflüssen weist darauf hin, daß viele der ursprünglichen architektonischen Vorstellungen des 20. Jahrhunderts zwar aus Europa kamen, aber in den Vereinigten Staaten erst eigentlich definiert und akzeptiert wurden. Obwohl Walter Gropius und Ludwig Mies van der Rohe in den Vereinigten Staaten lehrten und auf die amerikanische Architektur enormen Einfluß ausübten, setzten sich ihre sozialistischen Thesen dort nicht durch; selbst die von ihnen geschaffenen Formen erhielten durch die Anpassung an die Gegebenheiten dieses Landes eine typisch amerikanische Note.

Charakteristische Bauten

Die Entwicklung der amerikanischen Architektur läßt sich eher an einigen charakteristischen Bauten verfolgen als anhand von stark vereinfachten Generalisierungen. Dabei ergibt sich eine aktuelle Zustandsbeschreibung am ehesten aus der Summe der Beiträge ihrer herausragenden Vertreter. Allerdings entziehen sich die größten Künstler unter ihnen jeglicher Klassifizierung.

eering work of the Russian Constructivists seems inevitable, but unlike them, the Americans have the means to actually build their new world. Following Gehry's intellectual lead, younger architects such as Eric Owen Moss have begun to take on the basic expectations which exist about the built environment. There is a use of eccentric forms and materials in his work which often smacks of provocation, or even violent intent. At work here, as in much con-

pas racine et les formes auxquelles ils attachèrent leur nom n'ont pu prétendre à une qualité distinctement américaine qu'en s'adaptant aux exigences spécifiques de ce pays.

Bâtiments exemplaires

Le développement de l'architecture américaine se décrit mieux à travers des exemples concrets que par des généralisations forcément simplificatrices. L'image la plus précise de l'état actuel

temporary art, is the notion that standard esthetic views of beauty and/or harmony need to be aggressively rejected. Others, like Helmut Jahn, or Arquitectonica, have chosen to use the Modernist vocabulary in new ways. The maturity of these architects, as well as certain technical developments, permits them to distance themselves further from the doctrinaire Modernism born of the political ideals of the Bauhaus. In a recent building, Helmut Jahn, a native of Nuremberg who made his career in the United States, has come back to Germany not to praise the anonymous geometry of Bauhaus architecture, but rather to bury it. His Messeturm in Frankfurt am Main (1992) rejects the rectilinear design of so many modern skyscrapers, and takes on a more distinctive shape, reminiscent of New York's Art Deco towers of the late 1920's and early 1930's.

This trans-Atlantic shifting of shapes and influences points out that even if many of the original architectural ideas of the 20th century came from Europe, they were defined, and accepted in the United States. In any case, even if Walter Gropius or Ludwig Mies van der Rohe did teach in the United States and have an enormous impact on American architecture, their socialist theories, however, never took root there, and the forms they gave birth to assumed a distinctly American quality because of the specific requirements of the country in which they were built.

Mit Stick Style bzw. Shingle Style bezeichnete der Bauhistoriker Vincent Scully zwei Arten von Holzbauweisen, die der amerikanischen Architektur des 19. Jahrhunderts ein Moment der Originalität bescherten und als Grundlage zum besseren Verständnis zeitgenössischer Strömungen dienen können. Der Stick Style, charakterisiert durch steile Dächer und diagonale Verstrebungen, erreichte seinen Höhepunkt zwischen 1850 und 1875, wobei Griswold House (Newport, Rhode Island, 1863) von Richard Morris Hunt als hervorragendes Beispiel gelten kann. Der Shingle Style wurde um 1880 populär und zählte zu seinen bekanntesten Vertretern Pragmatiker wie H. H. Richardson und McKim, Mead and White. Dabei wurden gerade diese Architekten bekannt mit Gebäuden, die dem direkten Vergleich mit ihren Holzhäusern nicht standhielten. Dies gilt z. B. für die Trinity Church am Copley Square in Boston, die im Jahr 1872 nach einer erfolgreichen Ausschreibung in einem Stil erbaut wurde, der die Bezeichnung Richardsonsche Romanik erhielt. Auch heute noch wird Copley Square von dieser Kirche beherrscht, die sich mittlerweile jedoch im Schatten von Henry Cobbs John Hancock Tower (1966-76) befindet. Genau gegenüber dieser beiden Gebäude liegt die Boston Public Library, die zwischen 1888 und 1892 von McKim, Mead and White im Stile der Neorenaissance erbaut wurde. Der Shingle Style erlangte einige Bedeutung, denn, wie Vincent

de cette architecture sera ainsi la somme des contributions de ses créateurs les plus éminents, les plus grands artistes échappant comme toujours à toute classification.

Dans l'architecture américaine du XIX ème siècle, deux styles de construction en bois, baptisés par l'historien de l'architecture Vincent Scully le style «Stick» et le style «Shingle», se distinguent par leur originalité et permettent une meilleure appréciation des tendances contemporaines. Le style «Stick», caractérisé par des toits très pentus et des entretoises diagonales, a atteint son apogée entre 1850 et 1875. L'exemple le plus brillant étant Griswold House (Newport, Rhode Island, 1863) de Richard Morris Hunt. Le style «Shingle», quant à lui, devint à la mode vers 1880 et fit la gloire de praticiens comme H. H. Richardson ou McKim, Mead and White. En vérité, ces architectes signèrent aussi des édifices qui ne supportent pas la comparaison directe avec leurs maisons à structure de bois. Tel est le cas de l'église de la Sainte-Trinité dans le Copley Square à Boston, construite à l'issue d'un concours remporté en 1872 et dont le style fut qualifié de «roman richardsonien». Copley Square reste marqué par cette église, aujourd'hui à l'ombre de la John Hancock Tower (1966-76) d'Henry Cobb. Juste à l'opposé de ces deux bâtiments se trouve la Bibliothèque Publique de Boston, construite dans le style «Second retour à la Renaissance» par McKim, Mead and

Exemplary Buildings

The development of American architecture can perhaps better be traced through a certain number of specific cases, than through forcibly simplified generalisations. The most accurate image of the current state of architecture must be the sum of the contributions of outstanding creators. The greatest artists in any case defy classification.

Two styles of wooden construction, respectively named the Stick and Shingle Styles by the architectural historian Vincent Scully, offer glimpses of originiality in 19th century American architecture, and a better understanding of contemporary trends. The Stick Style, characterized by steep roofs and diagonal braces, reached its height between 1850 and 1875, with an outstanding example being the Griswold House (Newport, RI, 1863) by Richard Morris Hunt. The Shingle Style became fashionable towards 1880, and boasted such practitioners as H. H. Richardson and McKim, Mead, and White. In truth, these architects left their mark with buildings that did not bear direct comparison to their wooden frame houses. Such is the case with Trinity Church on Copley Square in Boston, built after a competition won in 1872, and whose style was dubbed Richardsonian Romanesque. Copley Square is still marked by this church, now in the shadow of Henry Cobb's John Hancock Tower (1966-76). Just opposite these

two buildings is the Boston Public Library, built in the style of the Second Renaissance Revival by McKim, Mead and White (1888-92). The Shingle Style certainly had repercussions, because, as Vincent Scully points out, »Frank Lloyd Wright's work grew directly out of the Shingle Style.« An example of this influence is the Frank Lloyd Wright House (Oak Park, IL, 1889).

Before commenting further on the seminal influence of Wright, which spans at least 70 years, it should be recalled that he began his career in the office of Louis Sullivan. Sullivan, like H. H. Richardson was present in Chicago, when it might be said that modern American architecture was invented. Richardson designed the Marshall Field Warehouse in 1885-87, the Walker Warehouse by Adler and Sullivan was completed two

Scully es ausdrückte: »Frank Lloyd Wrights Arbeiten hatten ihren Ursprung im Shingle Style.« Ein Beispiel für diesen Einfluß ist das Frank Lloyd Wright House (Oak Park, Illinois, 1889).

Aber vor weiteren Kommentaren zu Wrights folgenreichem Einfluß, der sich zumindest über eine Zeitspanne von 70 Jahren erstreckt, sollte daran erinnert werden, daß er seine Karriere im Büro von Louis Sullivan begann. Sullivan arbeitete ebenso wie H. H. Richardson zu einer Zeit in Chicago, von der man sagen könnte, daß dort die moderne amerikanische Architektur erfunden wurde. Zwischen 1885 und 1887 entwarf Richardson das Marshall Field Warehouse, und zwei Jahre später bauten Adler und Sullivan das Walker Warehouse. Es waren Burnham und Root, die einige der ersten Wolkenkratzer in Chicago bauten: das Montauk Building (1882), und beinahe ein Jahrzehnt später das Monadnock Building (1889-91). Noch modernere Konturen entstanden mit ihrem Reliance Building (1894-95). Chicago war aber auch die Stadt, in der William Le Baron Jenney mit seinem Home Insurance Building (1884-85) die Verwendung von Stahlträgern in der Architektur einführte. Louis Sullivans Meisterwerke, das Wainwright Building (St. Louis, Missouri, 1890-91), das Guaranty Building (Buffalo, New York, 1894-95) sowie sein vielleicht bedeutendstes Bauwerk, der Carson Pirie Scott Department Store (Chicago, Illinois, 1899-1904) legten den Grundstein für überraschend moderne

White (1888-92). Le style «Shingle» eut certainement des répercussions puisque, comme le fait remarquer Vincent Scully, «la maison de F. L. Wright à Oak Park, Illinois (1889) est un exemple de cette influence».

Avant de commenter davantage le rôle déterminant que Wright joua pendant au moins 70 ans, il est nécessaire de rappeler qu'il commença sa carrière dans le cabinet de Louis Sullivan. Sullivan, comme H. H. Richardson, était actif à Chicago au moment où il est convenu de dire que l'architecture américaine a été inventée. Richardson avait signé les Entrepôts Marshall Field en 1885-87 et Adler et Sullivan, deux ans plus tard, les Entrepôts Walker. Burnham et Root qui construisirent quelques-uns des premiers gratte-ciel de Chicago, le Montauk Building, en 1882, et le Monadnock

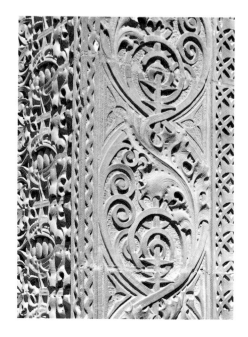

years later. It was Burnham and Root who built some of the first skyscrapers in Chicago, the Montauk Building in 1882 and the Monadnock Building almost a decade later (1889-91). An even more modern profile emerged with their Reliance Building (1894-95). Chicago was also the city where William Le Baron Jenney pioneered the use of steel beams in architecture with his Home Insurance Building (1884-85). Louis Sullivan's masterworks, the Wainwright Building (St Louis, MO, 1890-91), the Guaranty Building (Buffalo, NY, 1894-95), and perhaps most significant, the Carson Pirie Scott Department Store (Chicago, IL, 1899-1904), laid the foundations for strikingly modern and original architectural forms, which may never have reached their fullest expression. Louis Sullivan insisted, both in his built and written work, on the importance of ornament. Despite its clear horizontal bands, the Carson Pirie Scott store is festooned with decorative ironwork. Aside from Wright, few subsequent builders fully admitted that decorative elements could co-exist with modern architecture. Both of these figures proved that there was no contradiction between the two.

Wright and the 20th Century
H. H. Richardson also had an influence on the early work of Frank Lloyd Wright, as the proportions of the Heurtley House (Oak Park, IL, 1902) attest. But Wright quickly affirmed his own person-

und originelle architektonische Formen, die wohl nie ihre volle Ausdruckskraft erreicht haben. Sowohl in seinen Büchern als auch in seinen Werken bestand Louis Sullivan auf der Bedeutung des Ornaments. Das Carson Pirie Scott Gebäude ist trotz seiner klaren horizontalen Gliederung mit dekorativen Eisenornamenten geschmückt. Abgesehen von Wright waren nur wenige der nachfolgenden Architekten der Überzeugung, daß dekorative Elemente mit moderner Architektur vereinbar seien. Aber sowohl Sullivan als auch Wright haben bewiesen, daß es zwischen diesen beiden Komponenten keinen Widerspruch geben muß.

Wright und das 20. Jahrhundert
H. H. Richardson übte mit seinen Arbeiten großen Einfluß auf die frühen Projekte von Frank Lloyd Wright aus, wie die Proportionen des Heurtley House (Oak Park, Illinois, 1902) bestätigen. Aber mit Arbeiten wie dem Larkin Building (Buffalo, New York, 1904) oder dem Robie House (Chicago, Illinois, 1906-10) entwickelte Wright schnell eine eigene Persönlichkeit. Die langgestreckten Flügel des Robie House können im gleichen Maße als Symbol einer neuen, modernen Welt gesehen werden wie Picassos »Demoiselles d'Avignon«; aber seltsamerweise genießt ein Architekt in den Augen eines Kunsthistorikers nicht das gleiche Ansehen wie ein Maler. Dennoch vollzog sich in der Architektur ebenso wie in der Male-

Building, presque une décennie plus tard (1889-91). Chicago fut aussi la ville où William Le Baron Jenney utilisa pour la première fois dans l'histoire de l'architecture des poutres d'acier pour son Home Insurance Building (1884-85). Les chefs-d'œuvre de Louis Sullivan, le Wainwright Building (St-Louis, Missouri, 1890-91), le Guaranty Building (Buffalo, New York, 1894-95) et peut-être plus significativement encore les grands magasins Carson Pirie Scott (Chicago, Illinois, 1899-1904) introduisirent des formes architecturales franchement modernes et originales qui n'ont peut-être jamais atteint une expression plus accomplie. Louis Sullivan insistait par ailleurs dans ses œuvres construites comme dans ses écrits sur l'importance de l'ornementation. Malgré ses puissants bandeaux horizontaux, le magasin Carson Pirie Scott est festonné de ferronneries décoratives. Wright mis à part, peu de bâtisseurs admirent aussi clairement par la suite que des éléments décoratifs pouvaient coexister avec l'architecture moderne. Ces deux grands créateurs ont prouvé qu'il n'y avait pas là de contradiction.

Wright et le XXème siècle
H. H. Richardson exerça également une influence sur les premiers travaux de Frank Lloyd Wright comme en témoignent les proportions de sa Heurtley House (Oak Park, Illinois, 1902), mais Wright affirma rapidement sa propre personnalité à travers des réalisations

ality with works like the Larkin Building (Buffalo, NY, 1904), or the Robie House (Chicago, IL, 1906-10). The long, flat volumes of the Robie House should be considered as much of a symbol of the new, modern world as Picasso's »Demoiselles d'Avignon«, but somehow, for art historians, architects do not carry the same weight as painters. Much as in painting, however, the shift to modernity was accomplished not in a single leap, but bit by bit. At the same time that Wright was setting out on his own fundamentally personal path, others like the brothers Charles and Henry Greene were popularizing a type of wooden architecture which had great influence across the United States in the first twenty years of the century. Although they were imitated, few architects achieved the technical mastery which the Greene brothers showed in the David Gamble House (Pasadena, CA, 1908), for example.

One major event gave a hint of things to come in American architecture. That was the »Chicago Tribune« competition in 1922. Although the uninspired winner was a project by Hood and Howells, Adolf Loos participated with a sky-scraper-sized Doric Column, and, perhaps more significantly, Walter Gropius and Adolf Meyer submitted a remarkably powerful project not unrelated, as Vincent Scully pointed out, to the contemporary experiments of the Russian Constructivists and the De Stijl movement. Eliel Saarinen also participated in

rei der Wechsel zur Moderne nicht in einem großen Sprung, sondern in vielen kleinen Schritten. Zur gleichen Zeit, als Wright seinen eigenen Weg begann, machten andere, wie die Brüder Charles und Henry Greene, eine Holzbauweise populär, die in Amerika in den ersten zwanzig Jahren des Jahrhunderts großen Einfluß hatte. Obwohl man sie vielfach imitierte, erreichten nur wenige Architekten die technische Perfektion, durch die sich die Greene-Brüder z. B. in ihrem David Gamble House (Pasadena, California, 1908) auszeichneten.

Ein großes Ereignis warf seinen Schatten auf die kommenden Entwicklungen in der amerikanischen Architektur: die Ausschreibung der »Chicago Tribune« im Jahr 1922. Obwohl mit dem Projekt von Hood und Howells ein wenig aufregender Gewinner prämiert wurde, beteiligte sich Adolf Loos mit einer dorischen Säule vom Ausmaß eines Wolkenkratzers. Aber wahrscheinlich viel bedeutsamer war die Tatsache, daß Walter Gropius und Adolf Meyer einen bemerkenswert kraftvollen Entwurf vorstellten, der laut Vincent Scully Bezüge zu den zeitgenössischen Experimenten der russischen Konstruktivisten und zur De Stijl-Bewegung aufwies. Auch Eliel Saarinen nahm an der Ausschreibung mit einem Projekt teil, dessen aufstrebende vertikale Gliederung in den New Yorker Hochhäusern der dreißiger Jahre ein Echo gefunden zu haben scheint: Raymond Hoods Daily News Building (1930) und das symbolträchtige Empire

comme le Larkin Building (Buffalo, New York, 1904) ou la Robie House (Chicago, Illinois, 1906-10). Les volumes plats et allongés de la Robie House devraient être considérés comme annonciateurs d'un monde moderne alors en gestation au même titre que les «Demoiselles d'Avignon» de Picasso, mais pour les historiens d'art, d'une certaine façon, les architectes ne semblent pas avoir autant de poids que les peintres. Et pourtant, au moins autant qu'en peinture, le passage vers la modernité architecturale ne s'accomplit pas d'un seul coup mais petit à petit. Au moment même où Wright traçait un sillon éminemment personnel, d'autres, comme les frères Charles et Henry Greene popularisaient un type d'architecture en bois qui exerça une grande influence dans tous les Etats-Unis durant les vingt premières années de ce siècle. Bien qu'ils aient été beaucoup imités, peu d'architectes atteignirent la maîtrise technique des frères Greene tel qu'on peut l'observer dans la David Gamble House, par exemple (Pasadena, Californie, 1908).

Un événement majeur allait donner une idée plus précise du futur de l'architecture américaine. Ce fut le concours du «Chicago Tribune», de 1922. Même si le vainqueur fut le projet sans grande inspiration de Hood et Howells, Adolf Loos présenta un gratte-ciel en forme de colonne dorique, et plus significatif encore, Walter Gropius et Adolf Meyer soumirent un projet remarquablement puissant qui n'était pas sans relation avec

the competition with a project whose soaring vertical bands seem to have found an echo in the New York towers of the 1930's; Raymond Hood's Daily News Building (1930) or the symbolic Empire State Building (Shreve, Lamb and Harmon, New York, 1931). Although American skyscrapers may never again have achieved the variety of forms displayed throughout the 1920's and up to the Depression, the tall building remains a distinctly North American structural type. Chicago and New York gave examples to the rest of the world in a way which no other style of American architecture could, and this in spite of the number of Europeans who contributed to the evolution of the form. Simply put, with the development of the

State Building (Shreve, Lamb and Harmon, New York, 1931). Obwohl die amerikanischen Wolkenkratzer nie wieder eine solche Formenvielfalt erlangten, wie sie während der zwanziger Jahre bis zur Großen Depression entstand, stellen diese Hochhäuser nach wie vor eine typisch nordamerikanische Bauweise dar. Chicago und New York waren für den Rest der Welt in einer Art und Weise beispielhaft, die kein anderer amerikanischer Architekturstil jemals erreichte, und dies trotz der vielen europäischen Architekten, die zur Weiterentwicklung dieser Bauform beitrugen. Mit anderen Worten: die Entwicklung der Vereinigten Staaten erlaubte die Errichtung solcher neuen Städte, während man in Europa den historisch

les expériences contemporaines de l'avant-garde constructiviste russe et du mouvement De Stijl, comme le note Vincent Scully. Eliel Saarinen participa également à ce concours avec un projet dont les bandes verticales élancées semblent avoir trouvé un écho dans les tours new-yorkaises de Raymond Hood pour le «Daily News» (1930) ou le si emblématique Empire State Building (Shreve, Lamb and Harmon, New York, 1931). Même si les gratte-ciel américains ne retrouveront peut-être jamais la diversité formelle dont ils firent preuve tout au long des années vingt et jusqu'à la grande dépression, l'immeuble de grande hauteur reste une structure typiquement américaine. Chicago et New York donnèrent au reste du monde des leçons d'architecture qu'aucun autre style américain n'a égalé et ceci en dépit du nombre d'architectes européens qui contribuèrent à l'évolution de cette forme. Il se trouve simplement, qu'avec l'expansion accélérée des Etats-Unis, de nouvelles villes étaient à construire alors qu'en Europe, des constructions d'une telle envergure ne pouvaient être envisagées dans les centres historiques urbains, exception faite, après la Seconde Guerre mondiale, de quelques villes allemandes, comme Francfort-sur-le Main.

Au milieu de cette frénésie de construction urbaine, émergèrent deux styles dont l'origine était en partie européenne. Le premier était le style Art-Déco, issu de l'exposition de Paris de 1925 et

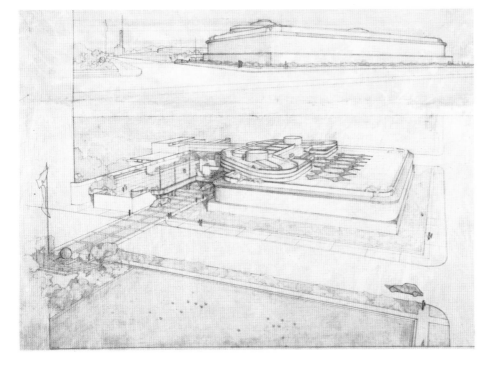

United States, new cities could be built, whereas in Europe, such wholesale construction could not be imposed on historic urban centers, with an exception to be made after World War II for some German cities such as Frankfurt/Main.

In the midst of this frenetic urban construction two styles – whose origin was at least partially European – came to the fore. The first of these was Art Deco, subsequent to the 1925 Paris exhibition, practiced by architects such as Ely Jacques Kahn in New York. It has been pointed out that American Art Deco surely owes some of its ornamental enthusiasm to Mayan or American Indian sources, as exemplified in Frank Lloyd

gewachsenen urbanen Zentren diese Einheitsbauweise nicht aufzwingen konnte; die Ausnahme bilden, bedingt durch den Zweiten Weltkrieg, einige deutsche Städte wie etwa Frankfurt am Main.

Inmitten dieses Baubooms traten zwei Stilrichtungen hervor, deren Wurzeln zumindest teilweise europäischer Herkunft waren. Bei der ersten handelte es sich um den Art deco, der im Anschluß an die Pariser Ausstellung des Jahres 1925 von Architekten wie Ely Jacques Kahn in New York eingeführt wurde. Zwar hat man darauf verwiesen, daß der amerikanische Art deco einen Teil seiner ornamentalen Verspieltheit mit Sicherheit indianischen oder Maya-Kulturen verdankt – wie in Frank Lloyd Wrights Barnsdall House (Hollywood, California, 1917-20) – dennoch kann die Dominanz des europäischen Einflusses nicht bezweifelt werden. Aufgrund seiner rein amerikanischen Ursprünge vielleicht noch interessanter ist der Streamline Trend, der nach 1930 aufkam und als ein erstes bewußtes Auflehnen gegen die Ornamentik gesehen werden kann. Ein hervorragendes Beispiel nicht nur für diesen Stil, sondern auch für die Originalität und Bedeutung des Werks von Frank Lloyd Wright bildet das S. C. Johnson and Son Company Administration Building (Racine, Wisconsin, 1936-39). Seine gestreifte horizontale Ausrichtung und die fließende Linienführung sind typisch für die Bauten der Streamline; aber dieses Gebäude wirkt auch heute

pratiqué par des architectes comme Ely Jacques Kahn à New York. Il a été relevé que l'Art-Déco américain devait certainement une part de son exhubérance décorative à des sources mayas ou indiennes, comme la Barnsdall House de Frank Lloyd Wright (Hollywood, Californie, 1917-20) en donne un bel exemple, mais il faut néanmoins reconnaître que l'influence européenne restait prédominante. Peut-être plus intéressant encore, de par ses racines plus locales, est la tendance «Streamline Moderne» qui débuta après 1930 et manifesta une première révolte contre l'ornement. Il est nécessaire de citer ici un immeuble majeur, non seulement pour illustrer ce mouvement, mais pour sa brillante démonstration de l'originalité et l'importance de l'œuvre de Frank Lloyd Wright. Il s'agit de l' immeuble de bureaux qu'il construisit pour S. C. Johnson & Son Company Administration Building (Racine, Wisconsin, 1936-39) et qui présente des surfaces courbes à larges bandeaux horizontaux, typiques du mouvement «Streamline». Presque soixante ans plus tard, cette structure demeure un témoignage de l'intemporalité que seul un grand architecte peut donner à l'expression d'une mode forcément datée. S'il est vrai qu'Erich Mendelsohn influença le développement de ce mouvement, Wright lui donna une expression qui ne pouvait être qu'américaine.

Le poids des influences artistiques est un facteur toujours assez complexe et nourrit à l'évidence et tout naturelle-

Wright's Barnsdall House (Hollywood, CA, 1917-20) but it is only fair to assume that European influence remained predominant. Perhaps even more interesting, because of its more American roots is the Streamline Moderne trend which began after 1930, and represented a first real revolt against ornament. One quintessential building must be cited here, not only as an example of this movement, but because it so fully demonstrates the originality and significance of the work of Frank Lloyd Wright. His S. C. Johnson & Son Company Administration Building (Racine, WI, 1936-39) shows the striped horizontality and curved surfaces typical of the Streamline movement. But this struc-

ture remains, almost 60 years later, a testimony to the timelessness that a great architect can give to an expression of current fashion. If it is true that Erich Mendelsohn influenced the development of the Streamline movement, Wright gave it an expression which is uniquely American.

noch, knapp 60 Jahre später, als Zeugnis einer Zeitlosigkeit, die nur ein großer Architekt einem Bauwerk im Stil der Zeit mitgeben kann. Während Erich Mendelsohn als entscheidender Einfluß bei der Entwicklung der Streamline gesehen wird, gab Wright dieser Bewegung eine Ausdruckskraft, die als spezifisch amerikanisch gelten kann.

Die Rolle des künstlerischen Einflusses ist im allgemeinen sehr komplex und natürlicher Bestandteil jeglicher Inspiration. Die Frage, wie der Architekt mit Einflüssen umgeht und was er daraus macht, ist der Schlüssel zur seiner Originalität und Bedeutung. Dies wurde deutlich, als in den Vereinigten Staaten die Vorherrschaft des International Style spürbar wurde. Von Ludwig Mies van der Rohe und Le Corbusier behauptete man beispielsweise, daß sie Frank Lloyd Wrights Entwurf für das berühmte Kaufmann House (Fallingwater, Bear Run, Pennsylvania, 1935-39) beeinflußt hätten. Aber Wright widerlegte in diesem, wie auch in vielen anderen Fällen, die Thesen seiner Kritiker durch seine pure Überlegenheit und architektonische Vision. Sowohl Mies van der Rohe als auch Le Corbusier vertraten eine puristische neue Vision der Architektur, die Le Corbusier sogar die Planierung ganzer Stadtteile in Paris erwägen ließ, um sie im Stil des Rationalismus wieder zu bebauen (Voisin Plan, 1925). Bei Fallingwater integrierte Wright eine auskragende Betonkonstruktion in eine natürliche Umgebung und bewies

ment ce qu'il est convenu d'appeler l'inspiration. Par contre, savoir ce qu'un architecte fait de ses influences est la clé de son originalité et de son apport. Ceci apparut avec clarté au fur et à mesure que se fit sentir la prédominance du Style International en Amérique. Il a été dit, par exemple, que Ludwig Mies van der Rohe et Le Corbusier auraient influencé la célèbre Kaufmann House (Fallingwater, Bear Run, Pennsylvanie, 1935-39) de Frank Lloyd Wright. Mais Wright, ici, comme dans de nombreux cas, confondit les critiques par sa maîtrise et la force de sa vision architecturale. Mies et Le Corbusier défendaient une vision pure de la nouvelle architecture qui, pour le second allait jusqu'à imaginer de raser une grande partie de Paris pour laisser place au modernisme du béton (Plan Voisin, 1925). A Fallingwater, Wright intègre une structure de béton en porte-à-faux dans un environnement naturel, prouvant que l'univers n'avait pas à être rasé pour faire place à l'architecture nouvelle. Il est intéressant de noter que cette maison fut construite presqu'en même temps que l'immeuble Johnson, ce qui prouve que Wright savait adapter son style en fonction des contraintes, aussi variées soient-elles.

Le Style International et le Modernisme

Le Style International qui allait dominer l'architecture du milieu de ce siècle fit son apparition aux Etats-Unis à la fin des années 20 à travers les travaux de deux

Ludwig Mies van der Rohe, Philip Johnson:
Seagram Building, New York, New York,
1954-58

The role of artistic influences is usually very complex, and indeed a natural part of any inspiration. The question of what an architect makes of influences is the key to his originality and importance. This was obvious as the predominance of the International Style began to be felt in the United States. It has been said, for example, that Ludwig Mies van der Rohe and Le Corbusier may have influenced Frank Lloyd Wright in his work on the famous Kaufmann House (Fallingwater, Bear Run, PA, 1935-39), but Wright here, as in many other cases, confounded the critics with his sheer mastery and architectural vision. Both Mies van der Rohe and Le Corbusier advocated a pure new vision of architecture, which for the latter even permitted the thought of razing large parts of Paris to accomodate concrete Modernism (Voisin Plan, 1925). With Fallingwater, Frank Lloyd Wright integrated a cantilevered concrete structure into a natural environment, proving that the world need not be flattened to make way for new architecture. Interestingly enough, Fallingwater was built almost at the same time as the S. C. Johnson & Son Company Administration Building.

The International Style and Modernism

The International Style, which was to dominate architecture at mid-century, arrived in the United States in the late 1920's with the work of two Austrians, Richard Neutra and Rudolph Schindler.

damit, daß die Welt nicht eingeebnet werden muß, um Platz für neue Architektur zu schaffen. Interessanterweise entstand Fallingwater etwa zur selben Zeit wie das S. C. Johnson & Son Company Administration Building, Beweis dafür, daß Wright seinen Stil den jeweiligen Umständen anpassen konnte.

Der International Style und die Moderne

Der International Style, der während der Mitte des 20. Jahrhunderts die gesamte Architektur beherrschen sollte, tauchte in den Vereinigten Staaten das erste Mal gegen Ende der zwanziger Jahre in den Projekten der beiden Österreicher Richard Neutra und Rudolph Schindler auf. Das von Neutra erbaute Lovell House (Los Angeles, California, 1929) und Schindlers Lovell Beach House (Newport Beach, California, 1925-26) zeugen von der strengen Formgebung, die dem europäischen und hauptsächlich deutschen Architekturverständnis entsprang, das Gropius, Mies van der Rohe und andere entwickelt hatten. Bereits im Jahr 1931 setzten die Architekten Howe und Lescaze den neuen International Style in einem großen Projekt um: dem Philadelphia Saving Fund Society Building. Im darauffolgenden Jahr veröffentlichten Henry-Russell Hitchcock und Philip Johnson ihr einflußreiches Werk »The International Style. Architecture since 1922« (dt. 1985) parallel zu Johnsons Ausstellung zu diesem

Autrichiens, Richard Neutra et Rudolph Schindler. La Lovell House (Los Angeles, Californie, 1929) construite par le premier et la Lovell Beach House (Newport Beach, Californie, 1925-26) par le second, présentent des formes rigoureuses nées d'une réflexion européenne et essentiellement allemande initiée par Gropius, Mies et quelques autres. C'est dès 1931 que les architectes Howe et Lescaze appliquèrent le Style International à un projet beaucoup plus vaste, le Philadelphia Saving Fund Society Building, et l'année suivante que le livre qui eut tant d'influence «The International Style. Architecture since 1922» fut publié par Henry-Russell Hitchcock et Philip Johnson en parallèle à l'exposi-

The Lovell House (Los Angeles, CA, 1929) built by the former, and the Lovell Beach House (Newport Beach, CA, 1925-26) built by the latter, show the rigorous forms born of European, and principally German architectural thought as developed by Gropius, Mies and others. As early as 1931, the architects Howe and Lescaze translated the new International Style into a larger structure with the Philadelphia Saving Fund Society Building, and the following year, the influential book »The International Style: Architecture since 1922« was published by Henry-Russell Hitchcock and Philip Johnson in connection with Johnson's show on the subject at the Museum of Modern Art. The urbane Johnson was to remain a central element in the acceptance of the International Style, through buildings such as his own Glass House (New Canaan, CT, 1949) or the superb Seagram Building (New York, 1954-58) on which he collaborated with Mies. Similarly, Gordon Bunshaft's Lever House (Skidmore, Owings and Merrill, New York, 1950-52) situated on Park Avenue, not far from where the Seagram Building was to rise, marked the definitive arrival of the International Style, with its sleek structure and »curtain wall« of glass, in the highest spheres of American corporate power. This transformation is more than a little surprising, when one takes into account the Socialist theories of the pre-War Bauhaus, but clearly, even though Gropius, Mies van der Rohe and Marcel

Thema im Museum of Modern Art. Der weltgewandte Johnson sollte zu einer zentralen Figur für die Akzeptanz des International Style werden, unter anderem durch Bauwerke wie etwa sein eigenes Haus, das Glass House (New Canaan, Connecticut, 1949) und das herausragende Seagram Building (New York, 1954-58), an dem er zusammen mit Mies van der Rohe arbeitete. In ähnlicher Weise kennzeichnet Gordon Bunshafts Lever House (Skidmore, Owings and Merrill, New York, 1950-52), das an der Park Avenue in der Nähe des später errichteten Seagram Building liegt, den endgültigen Durchbruch der eleganten Strukturen und gläsernen »Curtain walls« des International Style in die höchsten Sphären des amerikanischen Wirtschaftslebens. Dieser Sinneswandel erstaunt, wenn man die sozialistischen Theorien des Vorkriegs-Bauhaus bedenkt. Aber eines wird ganz deutlich: Obwohl Gropius, Mies van der Rohe und Marcel Breuer in die Vereinigten Staaten gingen, konnten sie nur Formen, aber keine Ideale importieren.
Eero Saarinen – Sohn von Eliel Saarinen und einer der Schüler Mies van der Rohes in den Vereinigten Staaten – entwarf zu Beginn seiner Laufbahn nur Gebäude, die eindeutig den Stempel seines Lehrers trugen, wie etwa das General Motors Technical Center (Warren, Michigan, 1948-56). Später entwickelte er eher lyrische Bauwerke wie das TWA Terminal auf dem Idlewild Airport (dem heutigen J. F. Kennedy International Air-

tion organisée par Johnson sur le même sujet au Museum of Modern Art. Très ouvert sur le monde, Johnson devait d'ailleurs demeurer l'un des principaux acteurs de la reconnaissance du Style International, à travers les projets comme la Glass House (New Canaan, Connecticut, 1949) qu'il construisit pour lui-même ou le superbe Seagram Building (New York, 1956-58) pour lequel il collabora avec Mies. La Lever House de Gordon Bunshaft (Skidmore, Owings and Merrill, New York, 1950-52) située sur Park Avenue, non loin du lieu où devait s'élever le Seagram Building, marqua la conquête définitive des sphères les plus élevées du pouvoir de l'Amérique des grandes entreprises par ce style, ses

Frank Lloyd Wright, Charles Gwathmey:
The Solomon R. Guggenheim Museum,
New York, New York, 1943-59, 1982-92

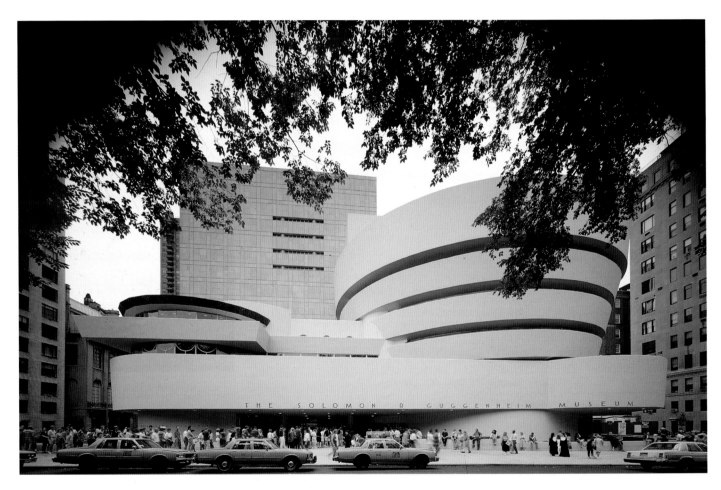

Breuer came to the United States, they succeeded in importing forms, but not ideals.

One disciple of Mies in the United States, Eero Saarinen, the son of Eliel Saarinen, at first designed buildings which bore the clear stamp of his teacher, such as the General Motors Technical Center (Warren, MI, 1948-56). He then embarked on more lyrical buildings like the TWA Terminal at Idlewild (now Kennedy) Airport (Long Island, NY, 1956-62), which bears a clear refer-

port, Long Island, New York, 1956-62), das an einen Vogel im Flug erinnert. Saarinens Büro wurde von Kevin Roche übernommen, der die Wende zu spektakulären Formen mit verschiedenen Bauwerken noch weiterführte: beispielsweise mit seinem Verwaltungsgebäude der Ford Foundation in New York (1963-68), dessen hochaufstrebende Innenräume einen enorm geräumigen Wintergarten umschließen.

Die These, daß der International Style die gesamte amerikanische Architektur

structures élancées et ses murs-rideaux de verre. Cette évolution n'étonne pas lorsqu'on se souvient des théories du Bauhaus d'avant-guerre. Même si Gropius, Mies van der Rohe et Marcel Breuer s'installèrent aux Etats-Unis et réussirent à importer leurs formes, ils échouèrent à faire partager leurs idéaux. Un des disciples de Mies aux Etats-Unis, Eero Saarinen, le fils d'Eliel Saarinen, débuta en dessinant des immeubles qui portaient clairement la marque du style de son professeur, comme le

ence to a bird in flight. The practice of Saarinen was to be taken over by Kevin Roche, who took the shift to spectacular form even further, with buildings like the Ford Foundation in New York (1963-68) whose soaring interior makes space for an enormous winter garden.

In fact, the idea that the pure International Style dominated American architecture in the 1950's might be said to be greatly exaggerated. Frank Lloyd Wright for one, continued his personal exploration with futuristic forms like those of Taliesin West (Maricopa Mesa, near Scottsdale, Arizona, 1937-59), or his controversial »inverted ziggurat« for the Guggenheim Museum (New York, 1943-59). Wright, in many ways one of the greatest artists of the 20th century, was not to leave as strong a mark on the American architecture of his time, as the immigrant Mies, perhaps because his quest was more protean and less systematic.

In the 1950's, Wright was of course at the end of his career. The man who may have inherited his mantle, at least in retrospect, as the most powerfully original and significant American architect was, appropiately enough, an immigrant. Louis Kahn's first major work was the New Art Gallery at Yale University (New Haven, CT, 1951-53), seen as a statement of the Brutalism which was to flourish in the following years. But Kahn, unlike some Brutalists, managed to suffuse his rough materials with a light and a sense of space which often

der fünfziger Jahre beherrscht habe, kann als grobe Übertreibung angesehen werden. Frank Lloyd Wright etwa setzte seine persönliche Entdeckungsreise fort, indem er futuristische Formen wie Taliesin West (Maricopa Mesa, nahe Scottsdale, Arizona, 1937-59) schuf oder seine umstrittene »auf den Kopf gestellte Zikkurat« für das Guggenheim Museum (New York, 1943-59). Wright, der in vielerlei Hinsicht zu den größten Künstlern des 20. Jahrhunderts zählt, konnte der amerikanischen Architektur seiner Zeit keinen so deutlichen Stempel aufdrücken wie der Immigrant Mies van der Rohe, vielleicht deshalb, weil sein Schaffen vielgestaltiger und weniger systematisch war.

In den fünfziger Jahren befand sich Wright schon am Ende seiner Karriere. Der Mann, der, zumindest in der Rückschau, am ehesten seine Nachfolge als bedeutendster und originellster amerikanischer Architekt hätte antreten können, war – natürlich – ein Immigrant. Louis Kahns erster großer Auftrag war die New Art Gallery der Yale University (New Haven, Connecticut, 1951-53), eine klare Manifestation des Brutalismus, der in den kommenden Jahren eine Blüte erleben sollte. Aber im Gegensatz zu verschiedenen anderen Brutalisten gelang es Kahn, seine rohen Materialien mit Licht und einem ans Mystische grenzenden Raumgefühl zu umgeben. Passenderweise trifft dies auch auf seine First Unitarian Church (Rochester, New York, 1959-67) zu. Noch beein-

General Motors Technical Center (Warren, Michigan, 1948-56) par exemple. Puis il se lança dans des projets plus lyriques comme le terminal TWA de l'aéroport d'Idlewild (aujourd'hui Kennedy, Long Island, New York, 1956-62) qui évoque un oiseau en vol. La clientèle de Saarinen devait être reprise par Kevin Roche qui poussa encore plus loin le caractère spectaculaire de ses formes dans des immeubles comme la Ford Foundation de New York (1963-68) dont le vertigineux espace intérieur abrite un énorme jardin d'hiver.

L'idée qu'un Style International pur ait pu dominer l'architecture américaine des années cinquante est en réalité très exagérée. Frank Lloyd Wright, par exemple, continua de son côté ses recherches futuristes comme à Taliesin West (Maricopa Mesa, près de Scottsdale, Arizona, 1937-59) ou dans sa très controversée «ziggourat inversée» du Guggenheim Museum (New York, 1943-59). Peut-être parce que sa quête était plus protéènne et moins systématique, Wright, qui reste à de multiples égards l'un des grands artistes du XX ème siècle, ne laissa sans doute pas une marque aussi forte sur l'architecture américaine de son temps que l'immigrant Mies van der Rohe.

Au cours des années cinquante, Wright était bien sûr à la fin de sa carrière. L'homme qui a peut-être hérité de lui de la couronne de l'architecte américain le plus fortement original et le plus significatif de son temps, du moins si l'on con-

border on the spiritual. This could be said, appropriately, of his First Unitarian Church (Rochester, NY, 1959-67). Even more impressive in their use of powerful geometries which bear little connection to the Miesian box, are Kahn's Second Capital of Pakistan (Dacca, East Pakistan, now Bangladesh, 1966), and his Indian Institute of Management (Ahmedabad, India, 1962-67). With the Jonas B. Salk Center for Biological Research (La Jolla, CA, 1959-65), and the later Kimbell Museum of Art (Fort Worth, TX, 1966-72) Louis Kahn earned a place in the list of the great architects of the century.

Using simple forms, the Kimbell Museum manages to highlight works of art in a way which few other modern archi-

druckender in der Verwendung kraftvoller geometrischer Formen, die nur wenig an Mies van der Rohes Kubusformen erinnern, sind Kahns Second Capital of Pakistan (Dacca, Ost-Pakistan, heute Bangladesh, 1966) und sein Indian Institute of Management (Ahmedabad, Indien, 1962-67). Mit dem Jonas B. Salk Center for Biological Research (La Jolla, California, 1959-65) sowie dem späteren Kimbell Museum of Art (Fort Worth, Texas, 1966-72) erwarb sich Kahn einen Platz in der Liste der größten Architekten dieses Jahrhunderts. Das von Kahn aus einfachen Formen erbaute Kimbell Museum präsentiert Kunstwerke in einer Art und Weise, wie es nur wenigen anderen modernen Architekten gelang. Die faßförmig gewölbten

sidère son parcours avec le recul du temps, fut, et il y a là encore une certaine logique, un immigrant. Première œuvre importante de Louis Kahn, la New Art Gallery de l'Université de Yale (New Haven, Connecticut, 1951-53), est une première pétition de principes du Brutalisme qui allait fleurir dans les années suivantes. Mais Kahn, à la différence de certains brutalistes, sut insuffler à ses matériaux bruts un sens de l'espace et de la lumière qui confine souvent à la spiritualité. On peut le dire à juste titre de sa First Unitarian Church (Rochester, New York, 1959-67). Plus impressionnante encore par son jeu puissant de géométries sans guère de rapports avec les «boîtes» de Mies est la seconde capitale du Pakistan, Dacca (1966, aujourd'hui au Bangladesh) et son Indian Institute of Management (Ahmedabad, Inde, 1962-67). Avec le Jonas B. Salk Center for Biological Research (La Jolla, Californie, 1959-65), et plus tard le Kimbell Museum of Art (Fort Worth, Texas, 1966-72), Louis Kahn ajouta son nom à la liste des grands architectes de ce siècle. Pour mettre en valeur les œuvres d'art – d'une façon dont peu d'architectes ont été capables – le Kimbell fait appel à des formes simples. Les voûtes en berceau des galeries, avec une seconde voûte intérieure qui oriente la forte lumière texane vers les œuvres tout en l'adoucissant, représentent une brillante solution au problème complexe de la lumière zénithale. En fait, l'architecture moderniste à son meilleur niveau n'a ja-

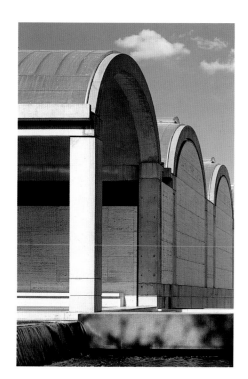

tects have been able to achieve. The barrel vaulted galleries, with a secondary inner vault carrying the bright Texas light down to the works and softening it at the same time, represent a brilliant solution to the problems of natural overhead lighting.

In fact, the best Modernist architecture did not represent a real abandonment of the principles which have historically informed the great buildings of all time. Walter Gropius ferociously willed the history of architecture and design to disappear. And as a matter of fact ornament has had a hard time of it since the days of Louis Sullivan and Frank Lloyd Wright. Modern construction techniques, based on pre-fabrication and assembly line production dovetailed nicely

Galerien mit ihrem zweiten, inneren Gewölbe lenken das strahlende texanische Licht auf die Kunstwerke und mildern es gleichzeitig – eine geniale Lösung für das komplexe Problem des natürlichen Lichteinfalls.

Tatsächlich verzichteten die besten Bauten der Moderne keineswegs auf die historisch gewachsenen Prinzipien, die allen großen Bauwerken vergangener Zeiten zu eigen sind. Gropius war wild entschlossen, die Geschichte der Architektur und des Designs zu beseitigen, und seit den Tagen von Louis Sullivan und Frank Lloyd Wright hatte das Ornament einen schweren Stand. Moderne Konstruktionstechniken, die auf vorgefertigten Bauteilen und Fließbandproduktion beruhten, paßten hervorragend zu den kubischen Formen, die von den Meistern des Bauhaus und ihren amerikanischen Jüngern heraufbeschworen wurden. Es war erheblich einfacher, identische Kastenformen aufeinanderzustapeln, als jede einzelne von ihnen zu variieren. Und dennoch konnten sich einige Architekten aus den formalen Zwänge früherer Zeiten befreien, indem sie auf verbesserte Herstellungsverfahren beim Formen und Gießen von Beton zurückgriffen. Philosophisch denkende Architekten wie Louis Kahn studierten mit besonderer Aufmerksamkeit die Baudenkmäler der Vergangenheit, und es gelang ihnen, die Essenz dessen herauszufiltern, was man wahrscheinlich als das »menschliche« Element aller großen Bauwerke bezeichnen kann: ih-

mais signifié l'abandon complet des principes à l'origine des plus grandes réussites architecturales de tous les temps, même si Gropius souhaita férocement la disparition de l'histoire de l'architecture et du design et si l'ornement connut des temps difficiles après Louis Sullivan et Frank Lloyd Wright. Les techniques modernes de construction, fondées sur la pré-fabrication et l'assemblage s'accordaient bien aux formes en boîte des maîtres du Bauhaus et de leur progéniture américaine. Il était beaucoup plus facile d'empiler des boîtes identiques les unes sur les autres que de différencier chacune d'entre elles. La mise au point de techniques plus sophistiquées de coulage et de mise en forme du béton libérèrent également certains architectes des contraintes formelles des périodes précédentes. Des architectes-penseurs comme Louis Kahn étudièrent les monuments du passé avec une attention particulière et surent en tirer l'essence même, qui est probablement le contenu humain de toutes les grandes constructions, leur grandeur et leur authenticité qui défie le temps. Vers le milieu des années soixante cependant, un besoin de réévaluation de l'architecture contemporaine commença à se faire sentir, du moins dans les cercles intellectuels.

Complexité et contradiction
Robert Venturi a été le premier de quelques architectes américains dont l'influence se fit sentir dans leurs écrits

with the box-like forms called up by the masters of the Bauhaus and their American progeny. It was much easier to pile identical boxes on top of each other than to differentiate each one. And yet the more sophisticated possibilities which developed for pouring and shaping concrete, also liberated some architects from the formal constraints of earlier times. Thinking architects like Louis Kahn studied the monuments of the past with particular attention, and managed to distill from them an essence, which is most probably the »human« content of all great buildings, their uplifting, timeless truth. And yet, by the mid 1960's, the need to reevaluate contemporary architecture began to make itself felt, at least in intellectual circles.

re erhabene, zeitlose Wahrheit. Dennoch wurde in der Mitte der sechziger Jahre, zumindest in intellektuellen Kreisen, der Wunsch nach einer Neubewertung der zeitgenössischen Architektur immer deutlicher spürbar.

Komplexität und Widerspruch

Robert Venturi war der erste einer Reihe von amerikanischen Architekten, der lange vor seinen ersten beachtenswerten Bauten durch seine Schriften Einfluß ausübte. Sein 1966 veröffentlichtes Buch »Complexity and Contradiction in Architecture« war die Losung für eine Generation, die von der reduzierenden Schlichtheit der Moderne endgültig genug hatte. Hier war ein Architekt, der sich nicht nur mit den barocken und manieristischen Meisterwerken Europas beschäftigte, sondern auch seine Ablehnung der kommerziellen nordamerikanischen Architektur zum Ausdruck brachte. Venturi erklärte die heroischen Absichten der Moderne für gescheitert, die zumindest in ihren Anfängen eine »Verbesserung« der Menschheit anstrebte. Wie die Protestbewegung gegen Ende der sechziger Jahre griff er das feste Gefüge des damaligen Establishments an. Was wir brauchen, erklärte Robert Venturi, ist eine Architektur, die »häßlich und gewöhnlich« ist. Er lobte Las Vegas und Los Angeles als würdige Prototypen und Inspirationsquelle für die Architektur von morgen. Eines wird hierbei ganz deutlich: der Berufsstand der Architekten wird in Ame-

avant qu'il n'aient pu construire quoi que ce soit de notable. Son livre de 1966, «Complexity and Contradiction in Architecture», fut le cri de ralliement d'une génération lassée de la simplicité réductrice du Modernisme. Survenait enfin un architecte qui analysait non seulement les chefs-d'œuvre baroques ou maniéristes européens mais, presque avec incongruité, se penchait aussi sur l'architecture commerciale américaine. Venturi déclarait que les héroïques prétentions du Modernisme, qui avait eu au moins le mérite de chercher à faire le bien de l'humanité, étaient mortes. Comme les contestataires de la fin des années 60, il s'attaquait à tout l'édifice de l'establishment contemporain. Ce dont nous avons besoin, déclara-t-il, c'est d'une architecture «laide et ordinaire». Il fit le panégyrique de Las Vegas et de Los Angeles promues sources d'inspiration pour l'architecture du futur. Un de ses arguments semble ici pertinent: la profession d'architecte, et en Amérique plus que dans d'autres pays, n'est pas dominée par des célébrités du niveau de Wright ou de Kahn, mais plutôt par de grands cabinets anonymes qui réalisent les innombrables centres commerciaux, immeubles de bureaux et alignements de maisons individuelles qui sont le vrai visage de l'architecture américaine.

Il faut enfin noter que les positions théoriques que Venturi essaya de mettre en pratique aux débuts de sa carrière se sont récemment heurtées aux désirs de

Complexity and Contradiction

Robert Venturi was the first of several American architects whose influence was felt in written form, before he really built much which was worthy of notice. But his 1966 book, »Complexity and Contradiction in Architecture« was the rallying call for a generation which had had enough of the reductive simplicity of Modernism. Here was an architect who looked not only at the Baroque and Mannerist masterpieces of Europe, but, almost incongruously, at the commercial architecture of the United States. Venturi declared the heroic pretensions of Modernism, which at least at the outset had sought to »improve« mankind, to be dead. Like the protesters of the late 1960's, he attacked the edifice of the contemporary establishment. What we needed, declared Robert Venturi, was an architecture which is »ugly and

rika – noch deutlicher als in einigen anderen Ländern – keineswegs von vergleichbaren Koryphäen wie Wright oder Kahn beherrscht. Es sind vielmehr die großen kommerziellen Büros, die am laufenden Band Einkaufszentren, Bürogebäude und Reihenhäuser produzieren und damit Amerikas Gesicht wirklich prägen.

Interessanterweise mußten allerdings Robert Venturis Theorien, die er zu Beginn seiner Karriere in die Praxis umzusetzen versuchte, vor nicht allzu langer Zeit dem Wunsch der Klientel nach weniger unattraktiven Gebäuden Platz machen. Als man Neil MacGregor, den Direktor der National Gallery in London, nach seiner Meinung bezüglich Venturis Maxime der Sechziger befragte – Architektur müsse »häßlich und gewöhnlich« sein – antwortete er, er hoffe, daß das Publikum Venturis Erweiterungsbau des Museums, den Sainsbury Wing (1991), »schön und außergewöhnlich« finden werde.

Möglicherweise war die Gründung der »New York Five«, einer Gruppe junger Architekten zu Beginn der siebziger Jahre, eine Reaktion auf die Verzerrung der ursprünglichen Ideale der Moderne und auf Venturis Revisionismus. Die Mitglieder dieser Gruppe – Richard Meier, John Hejduk, Michael Graves, Peter Eisenman und Charles Gwathmey – veröffentlichten 1972 ein Buch mit dem einfallsreichen Titel »Five Architects«, das ihre Auffassung von der Rückkehr zu den Vorgaben Le Corbusiers deutlich

clients potentiels souhaitant quelque chose de plus passionnant que des bâtiments sans le moindre attrait. Quand on lui demanda ce qu'il pensait de la déclaration de Venturi des années 60 selon laquelle l'architecture devait être «laide et ordinaire», Neil McGregor, Directeur de la National Gallery de Londres, répondit qu'il espérait que le public trouverait la nouvelle Sainsbury Wing, l'extension du musée, réalisée par Venturi en 1991: «Superbe et exceptionnelle».

C'est peut-être en réaction aux déformations des idéaux originels du Modernisme et au révisionnisme de Venturi que se constitua au début des années 70 un groupe de jeunes architectes, les «New York Five» (les «Cinq de New York»), composé de Richard Meier, John Hejduk, Michael Graves, Peter Ei-

Robert A. M. Stern: The Norman Rockwell
Museum, Stockbridge, Massachusetts,
1987-92

ordinary«. He praised Las Vegas and Los Angeles as prototypes worthy of inspiring the architecture of the future. One point made here seems obvious – the architectural profession, in America more than in some other countries, is not truly dominated by the likes of Wright or Kahn. Rather it is the large commercial offices that churn out shopping centers, office buildings, and row houses that really shape the face of American architecture.

It is interesting to note that the theoretical positions of Robert Venturi, which he did try to put into practice early in his building career, have more recently come up against the desire of clients to have something other than an unattractive building. When asked what he thought about Venturi's 1960's maxim that architecture should be »ugly and ordinary,« Neil MacGregor, the Director of London's National Gallery, said that he hoped the public would find Venturi's

machte. In Anspielung auf die vorherrschende Farbe ihrer Werke auch »The Whites« genannt, blieben die Theorien der New York Five – in besonderem Maße von Eisenman und Hejduk, die während der siebziger und frühen achtziger Jahre relativ wenig bauten – auch in den folgenden Jahren von Bedeutung. Diese von zeitgenössischer französischer Philosophie beeinflußten Vordenker betrachteten sich selbst gerne als Baumeister einer vollkommenen neuen Analyse der Architektur. Ihr Status als Theoretiker ist ein neues Phänomen in der Architekturgeschichte. Denn andere Vordenker wie etwa einige der französischen Revolutionsarchitekten oder die Mitglieder der russischen Avantgarde hatten niemals die Gelegenheit, ihre gezeichneten Projekte in die Wirklichkeit umzusetzen – dennoch dachten sie hauptsächlich in architektonischen Begriffen. Die New Yorker dagegen erweckten den Anschein, daß

senman et Charles Gwathmey. En 1972, ils publièrent un livre sous le titre sans grande imagination de «Cinq Architectes», qui proposait un retour aux prémisses de l'œuvre de Le Corbusier. Surnommés les «Whites» (les «Blancs», pour la couleur dominante de leurs projets), les New York Five constituèrent un noyau théorique très présent, en particulier grâce à Eisenman ou Hejduk qui ne construisirent que très peu pendant les années 70 et jusqu'au début des années 80. Souvent influencés par la philosophie contemporaine française, ils aimaient à penser qu'ils jetaient les bases d'une analyse nouvelle et approfondie de l'architecture. Leur statut de théoriciens peut être considéré comme un phénomène nouveau en architecture. D'autres, comme certains des architectes français de la Révolution ou de l'avant-garde russe, n'eurent jamais la chance de mener à bien leurs projets qui restèrent sur le

Sainsbury Wing (1991) extension to the museum »beautiful and exceptional.«

It may have been as a reaction to the deformation of the original ideals of Modernism, and to the revisionism of Venturi, that a group of young architects was formed in the early 1970's. The so-called »New York Five«, consisting of Richard Meier, John Hejduk, Michael Graves, Peter Eisenman, and Charles

ein paar Ideen genügten, um zum »Star« der zeitgenössischen Architektur ernannt zu werden.

Erst spät, vielleicht zu spät im Laufe seiner Karriere entdeckte beispielsweise Peter Eisenmann gegen Ende der achtziger Jahre, daß es sehr frustrierend ist, dem Rest der Welt zu erzählen, wie man zu bauen habe, ohne sich dabei jemals selbst die Hände schmutzig gemacht zu haben – vielleicht hat ihm dies aber auch sein Psychoanalytiker gesagt; auf jeden Fall begann er gehorsam zu bauen.

Richard Meiers High Museum (Atlanta, 1980-83) und das von ihm entworfene Museum für Kunsthandwerk in Frankfurt am Main (1979-84) bestätigen die nach wie vor vorhandene Vitalität der Ideale der New York Five. Während Meier sich in seinen zahlreichen weißen modernistischen Gebäuden eine kämpferische Reinheit erhielt, muß Michael Graves mit seinen mediterranen Farben und seiner italianisierten Postmoderne auf seinem Weg zum Ruhm während der achtziger Jahre ein wenig vom eigentlichen Ziel abgewichen sein. Der eher handwerkliche und beständige Charles Gwathmey widmete sich 1982-92 in liebevoller Arbeit der Restaurierung von Frank Lloyd Wrights Guggenheim Museum und fügte einen blockförmigen Turm hinzu, den sein Mentor Le Corbusier sicher begrüßt hätte. Dieser offensichtliche Widerspruch ist typisch für das Schicksal der Theorien der New York Five.

papier mais ils pensaient néanmoins surtout en terme de construction. Les New Yorkais semblaient suggérer que pour être une «star» de l'architecture contemporaine, il suffisait d'avoir quelques idées.

Un peu tardivement, Peter Eisenman entre autres, découvrit à la fin des années 80 qu'il était très frustrant d'apprendre au reste du monde comment construire sans réellement se salir les mains (ou du moins c'est ce que lui expliqua son psychanalyste) et obéissant, ilse mit à construire.

Le High Museum (Atlanta, 1980-83) de Richard Meier ou son Musée des Arts Décoratifs de Francfort-sur-le Main (1979-84) affirment la permanence de la vitalité des idéaux des New York Five. Mais si Meier maintint une pureté de chevalier croisé dans ses nombreuses constructions blanches et modernistes, Michael Graves, un autre membre des New York Five, à partir d'un certain moment s'en éloigna à une vitesse vertigineuse et devint l'adepte des couleurs méditerranéennes et du postmodernisme italianisant qui marquèrent sa montée vers la célébrité.

Charles Gwathmey, plus travailleur et plus fidèle, restaura avec amour le Guggenheim Museum de Frank Lloyd Wright en 1992, en lui ajoutant une tour rectangulaire que Le Corbusier, son mentor, n'aurait peut-être pas désavouée. Cette contradiction apparente fut en fait assez typique du destin des théories des New York Five.

Gwathmey, published a book in 1972 under the imaginative title »Five Architects«, which outlined their idea of a return to the premises of the work of Le Corbusier. Nick-named »The Whites« because of the dominant color of their work, the New York Five remained an important theoretical presence, especially through Eisenman and Hejduk, who did very little actual building throughout the 1970's and early 1980's. Often influenced by contemporary French philosophy, these were the thinkers who liked to see themselves as laying the groundwork for a profound new

Neo-Modernismus und Postmodernismus

Wie so oft in der amerikanischen Architektur gab es mindestens zwei Strömungen, die Venturis Ideen weiterführten. Die erste dieser Stilrichtungen hat mit den Theorien des Professors an der Universität von Philadelphia nur wenig zu tun und entsprang eher dem Glauben, daß der Modernismus sein Ende noch nicht erreicht habe. Neben den bereits erwähnten New York Five bedienen sich I. M. Pei, Cesar Pelli, Paul Rudolph und Edward Larrabee Barnes bis heute einer Formgebung, die mehr der Zeit unmittelbar nach dem Modernismus zuzuschreiben ist als den weiter zurückliegenden Stilrichtungen, deren Gedankengut eine Zeit lang von den Verfechtern des Postmodernismus weiterverbreitet wurde. Peis East Building der National Gallery of Art (Washington, D. C., 1978) erforscht die Möglichkeiten, die die Dreiecksform der Architektur bietet. Neben John Russell Popes Gebäude aus den dreißiger Jahren, in der Nähe des Capitol auf einer dreieckigen Parzelle gelegen, ist das East Building mit seinen dramatischen Kanten und seinem lichtdurchfluteten Atrium sicherlich mehr als nur eine Neuauflage modernistischer Ideen. Es liefert den Beweis für die Vitalität einer dynamischen, geometrischen Architektur, und ist doch fast völlig frei von Ornamenten und historischen Bezügen. Mit dem Entschluß, im Hof des Louvre eine Pyramide zu errichten, wandte sich Pei zu Be-

Néo-moderne et post-moderne

Comme c'est souvent le cas dans l'architecture américaine, deux mouvements au moins apparurent à la suite du brûlot de Venturi. Le premier devait assez peu aux pensées du professeur de Philadelphie et davantage à la croyance que le Modernisme n'avait pas encore dit son dernier mot. A ce jour, à côté des New York Five mentionnés plus haut, I. M. Pei, Cesar Pelli, Paul Rudolph ou Edward Larrabee Barnes pratiquent des formes qui doivent plus au passé immédiat du Modernisme qu'aux échos plus distants de l'histoire de l'architecture exploités, du moins pendant quelques années, par les défenseurs du post-modernisme. L'East Building de la National Gallery of Art de Pei (Washington, D. C., 1978) est une exploration des possibilités offertes à l'architecture par le triangle. Situé sur un terrain triangulaire tout près des bâtiments des années 30 de John Russell Pope et non loin du Capitole, cet édifice, avec ses angles dramatiques et son atrium saturé de lumière, est certainement bien plus qu'une simple application de principes modernistes. Il est la preuve de la vitalité d'une architecture dynamique, d'esprit géométrique, libéré de tout ornement ou de toute référence historique. En choisissant de construire une pyramide dans la cour du Louvre au début des annés 80, Pei se rapprocha des théories du célèbre créateur de jardins à la française, Le Nôtre, qui disait que le ciel et l'eau étaient les principales composantes de

analysis of architecture. Their status, as theoreticians might be considered a new phenomenon in the history of architecture. Others, like some of the French Revolutionary architects, or the Russian avant-garde, never had a chance to build the works they drew on paper – but they still thought mainly in terms of buildings. The New Yorkers seemed to suggest that to be a »star« of contemporary architecture, it sufficed to have some ideas. A little late in his career, Peter Eisenman, for one, discovered in the late 1980's that it was very frustrating to tell the rest of the world how to build without actually getting your own hands dirty – or so his psychoanalyst told him, and he obediently began to build. Richard Meier's High Museum (Atlanta, GA, 1980-83), or his Museum for the Decorative Arts (Frankfurt, Germany, 1979-84) affirm the continuing vitality of

ginn der achtziger Jahre den Ideen des berühmten französischen Gartenarchitekten Le Nôtre zu, der Himmel und Wasser als die Grundelemente seiner Entwürfe bezeichnete. Wenn sich der Modernismus im späten 20. Jahrhundert auf solche historischen Persönlichkeiten beziehen kann, ist seine Lebensdauer wahrscheinlich länger als erwartet. Tatsächlich ist Peis Identifikation mit Le Nôtres »Minimalismus« bezeichnend für einen Trend zu subtileren oder tiefgründigeren historischen Bezügen, nach denen heute die Architekten suchen, die man als »Neo-Modernisten« bezeichnet.

Peis Beitrag zur zeitgenössischen amerikanischen Architektur umfaßt immer auch die Arbeit seiner beiden wichtigsten Partner, Henry Cobb und James Ingo Freed. Tatsächlich war es Cobb, von dem der Entwurf zum John Hancock Tower am Copley Square in Boston stammt, der trotz einiger technischer Probleme zu den erfolgreichsten Wolkenkratzern der vergangenen 25 Jahre zählt. James Ingo Freed – 1939 als Flüchtling aus Deutschland in die Vereinigten Staaten eingewandert – ist der Erbauer des New York Convention Center (1985), aber sein Meisterwerk stammt aus jüngerer Zeit: das Holocaust Memorial in Washington, D. C. (1993). Dieses Bauwerk verschmilzt und löst die offensichtlich widersprüchlichen Tendenzen historischer Anspielungen, die sich auf die unmittelbare Umgebung, die Industriearchitektur,

ses créations. Si le Modernisme de la fin du XXème siècle peut se prévaloir de telles références historiques, sa durée de vie sera sans doute plus longue qu'on ne le pensait. En fait, l'identification de Pei au «minimalisme» de Le Nôtre témoigne d'une tendance à la prise en compte de sources historiques plus subtiles et plus profondes illustrée aujourd'hui par des architectes qui peuvent être qualifiés «Néo-modernistes». Il faut noter que la contribution de Pei à l'architecture américaine contemporaine comprend également les noms de ses deux principaux associés, Henry Cobb et James Ingo Freed. Ce fut Cobb qui dessina la John Hancock Tower de Copley Square, à Boston, qui, malgré quelques problèmes d'ingéniérie s'est affirmée comme l'un des gratte-ciel les plus réussis de ce dernier quart de siècle. James Ingo Freed, qui venu d'Allemagne se réfugia aux Etats-Unis en 1939, a édifié le New York Convention Center (1985) mais son chef-d'œuvre, l'Holocaust Memorial de Washington, D. C., est encore plus récent (1993). Cette construction mêle et apparemment résout les contradictions apparentes de courants aux références historiques multiples, tels que l'architecture industrielle, le Modernisme et les dislocations violentes du déconstructivisme. En tant que tel, il est l'un des témoins architecturaux essentiels des années 90, car il véhicule également, à sa façon, le malaise d'une époque de grande incertitude économique et spirituelle.

James Ingo Freed: Holocaust Memorial,
Washington, D. C., 1993

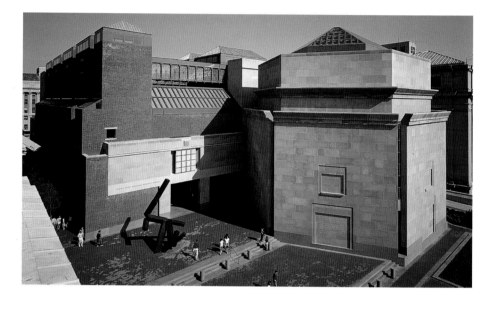

the ideals of the New York Five. But if Meier retained a crusading purity in his many white, Modernist buildings, Michael Graves must have somewhere gone astray with the Mediterranean colors and Italianate Post-Modernism of his 1980's rise to celebrity. Gwathmey, more workman-like and consistent, went on to lovingly restore Frank Lloyd Wright's Guggenheim Museum in 1992, adding a block-shaped tower of which his mentor Le Corbusier might not have disapproved. This apparent contradiction actually was quite typical of the fate of the theories of the New York Five.

Neo-Modern and Post-Modern

As is often the case in American architecture, at least two trends were carried forward after Venturi's battle cry. The first of these owed little to the Philadelphia professor's thoughts, and rather more to the belief that Modernism had not yet run its course. Aside from the New York Five mentioned above, to this day, I. M. Pei, Cesar Pelli, Paul Rudolph and Edward Larrabee Barnes, practice in forms which owe more to the immediate Modernist past than to the more distant echoes sought out, at least for a few years by the defenders of Post-Modernism. Pei's East Building for the National Gallery of Art (Washington, D. C., 1968-78) is an exploration of the possibilities offered to architecture by the triangle. Situated on a triangular lot next to John Russell Pope's 1930's building, and not far from the Capitol,

den Modernismus und die gewundenen Verrenkungen des Dekonstruktivismus beziehen. In dieser Hinsicht ist es eines der wichtigsten Bauten der neunziger Jahre, da es auch die »malaise« einer Zeit wirtschaftlicher und geistiger Unsicherheiten verdeutlicht.

Eine andere wichtige Strömung innerhalb der modernen amerikanischen Architektur nähert sich aus naheliegenden Gründen ihrem Ende. Durch den Verrat an den Idealen der »Whites« – durch Michael Graves und Robert A. M. Stern oder den allgegenwärtigen Philip Johnson – wurde die Idee, daß bestimmte historische Formen zumindest die Fassaden moderner Gebäude auflockern könnten, mehr und mehr akzeptiert. Graves' Public Services Building (Portland, Oregon, 1980-82) war das erste große Bauwerk, das diese Ästhetik übernahm: zu erkennen an dem Farb-

Une autre grande tendance de l'architecture américaine récente est actuellement en voie d'extinction, et ce pour des raisons évidentes. A travers les œuvres de ce «traître» aux idéaux des «Whites», Michael Graves, et de Robert A. M. Stern, ou du toujours présent Philip Johnson, l'idée que certaines formes historiques pouvaient animer ne serait-ce que les façades des immeubles modernes se fraya son chemin. Le Public Services Building de Graves (Portland, Oregon, 1980-82) fut la première structure de grande dimension à adopter cette esthétique, dont l'apport était évident dans la coloration pastel ou les sculptures ornementales prévues, mais qui ne fut jamais terminée. Son Humana Building (Louisville, Kentucky, 1982-86) confirma et amplifia le message. Le AT&T Building de Philip Johnson (New York, 1978-82) prouva que la seule adjonction

ing, with all of the amenities of the day of course. The exaggerated forms and Pompeian colors employed by these architects make their work of the late 1970's and 1980's look very dated today. Another adaptable, but more overtly humoristic architect, Charles Moore, survived the general disaffection with the Post-Modern which emerged in the late 1980's. Moore's Piazza d'Italia (New Orleans, LA, 1977-78) is so much of a caricature of Italian architecture that it becomes an agreeable sort of theatre decor for the urban environment, but his recent work, such as the Tegel Harbor Housing project (Berlin, 1987) looks much more serious.

As is usually the case, the major trends in American architecture co-exist with more eccentric visions. The late Bruce Goff and his disciple Bart Prince, for example, might be said in a way to have carried forward the originality of some of Frank Lloyd Wright's houses. James Wines and his Site group are also representative of the vitality of marginal architects in America. For a number of years, his emphasis on the integration of nature into the urban environment went unheeded, but with environmentalism on the rise, projects such as Site's Avenue 5 (Seville Universal Exhibition, 1992) seem to be closer to main-stream thought. Environmentally responsible architecture is certainly one of the rallying calls of the early 1990's, and other architects can be expected to complete »green« buildings in the near future.

Der verstorbene Architekt Bruce Goff und sein Schüler Bart Prince beispielsweise haben in gewisser Hinsicht die Originalität einiger Häuser von Frank Lloyd Wright fortgeführt. James Wines und seine Site-Gruppe sind ebenfalls beispielhaft für die Vitalität einer Randgruppe innerhalb der amerikanischen Architektengemeinschaft. Mehrere Jahre fand Wines These von der Integration der Natur in eine urbane Umgebung keine Beachtung, aber mit dem Aufkommen der Umweltschutzbewegung rückten diese Projekte wie Sites Avenue 5 (Expo, Sevilla, 1992) näher an den Puls der Zeit. Umweltbewußte Architektur ist zweifelsohne eines der Schlagworte der frühen neunziger Jahre, und sicherlich werden in naher Zukunft andere Architekten die »grünen« Gebäude vervollkommnen.

d'année, l'accent qu'il mettait sur l'intégration de la nature dans l'environnement urbain fut assez peu remarqué, mais avec le succès des préoccupations écologiques, des projets comme celui de Site pour l'Avenue 5 (Seville, Expo'92) semblent maintenant faire partie d'un mouvement de fond. L'architecture d'esprit écologique est certainement l'une des tendances montantes du début des années 90 et d'autres architectes proposeront certainement des immeubles «verts» dans un proche futur.

Déconstruction et années 90

Si les survivants du Post-modernisme continuent à travailler et si de sérieux immeubles néo-modernes sont toujours appréciés, les années 90 ont cependant débuté par un autre défi. Avec Frank Gehry en tête, et des architectes

Frank O. Gehry: American Center (model),
Paris, France, 1990; Walt Disney Concert
Hall (model), Los Angeles, California, 1992

Deconstruction and the 1990's

With remnants of the Post-Modern continuing to exist, and strongly Neo-Modern buildings still being designed, the 1990's have begun with yet another challenge to the established order. With Frank Gehry in the lead, and more theoretical architects like Peter Eisenman, ex-member of the New York Five, following in even more radical departures from traditional forms, a trend that can largely be labeled Deconstructivism has begun to take hold. The rectilinear

Dekonstruktivismus und die neunziger Jahre

Obwohl die Überreste des Postmodernismus noch existieren und immer noch kraftvolle neo-modernistische Gebäude entworfen werden, bilden die neunziger Jahre eine weitere Herausforderung an die festgefahrenen Ansichten des Establishments. Mit Frank Gehry an der Spitze, gefolgt von anderen eher theoretisch orientierten Architekten wie Peter Eisenman (dem ehemaligen Mitglied der New York Five), die sich noch radika-

plus théoriciens comme Peter Eisenman, ex-membre des New York Five, s'orientant vers des ruptures encore plus radicales par rapport aux formes traditionnelles, une tendance qui peut être étiquetée de façon générique comme déconstructiviste a commencé à se faire jour. Les formes raides du Modernisme et même les élégantes harmonies de ses variantes les plus récentes semblent pouvoir être balayées par ces architectes dont les réalisations paraissent plus prêtes à tomber en morceaux qu'à s'élever avec grâce. Peter Eisenman n'appelle à rien moins qu'une réévaluation de la façon dont l'espace est dessiné et réparti dans une construction. Il en donne un exemple dans son modèle «cristallin», créé à l'aide d'un ordinateur pour la Max Reinhardt Haus (Berlin, 1992). La référence historique, en particulier sous la forme d'un décor appliqué est rejetée avec force par ce mouvement qui n'est pas sans quelque ressemblance, néanmoins, avec certaines fantaisies architecturales des constructivistes russes. Malgré la contribution active à cette tendance de groupes européens comme les Autrichiens de Coop Himmelblau, l'Amérique semble être à la tête de ce mouvement.

Il reste à voir si ces principes déconstructivistes révolutionnaires pourront influer sur le cours prépondérant de l'architecture des Etats-Unis. Frank Gehry paraît déjà y avoir réussi, à sa façon très personnelle, avec des commandes im-

shapes of Modernism and even the harmonies of its more recent variants look as though they might be swept aside by architects whose buildings seem more like they are falling apart rather than standing up with ease. Peter Eisenman calls for no less than a reevaluation of the way space is designed and alloted in a building, as exemplified in his crystalline model, created with the aid of a computer, for the Max Reinhardt Haus (Berlin, 1992). Historic reference, especially in the form of an applied decor is aggressively rejected by this trend, which nonetheless bears more than a passing resemblance to the architectural fantasies of the Russian Constructivists. Despite the active contribution of European groups like the Austrians Coop Himmelblau to the development of these trends, Americans seem to lead in its evolution.

It remains to be seen if the revolutionary principles of Deconstructivist architecture can enter the mainstream in the United States. Frank Gehry seems already to have accomplished just that, in his very personal way, with his large scale commissions for the Walt Disney Concert Hall in Los Angeles, or the American Center in Paris. The latter project, situated on the Right Bank, near the new Ministry of Finance at Bercy, and just opposite the Bibliothèque de France building, was designed from the inside out. A street-side façade gives no clue of the unusual uses of space that Gehry has invented for this complex

ler von den traditionellen Formen abwenden, faßt ein Trend Fuß, der als Dekonstruktivismus bezeichnet werden kann. Es hat den Anschein, als ob die geradlinigen Formen der Moderne und selbst die harmonischen Konturen ihrer jüngeren Varianten von Architekten hinweggefegt würden, deren Bauwerke eher zusammengestückelt als sorgfältig konstruiert wirken. Peter Eisenman fordert nichts weniger als ein völliges Umdenken bei der Raumaufteilung von Gebäuden, wie sein Kristallmodell verdeutlicht, das er mit Hilfe eines Computers für das Max Reinhardt Haus (Berlin, 1992) entwickelte. Historische Bezüge – besonders in Form von Fassadenelementen – werden von dieser Strömung heftig abgelehnt, obwohl sie mehr als nur eine flüchtige Ähnlichkeit mit den Phantasien der russischen Konstruktivisten aufweist. Trotz der europäischen Mitwirkung bei der Entwicklung dieser Trends – wie z. B. Coop Himmelblau aus Österreich – scheint Amerika diese Entwicklung anzuführen.

Es bleibt abzuwarten, ob die revolutionären Prinzipien der dekonstruktivistischen Architektur in die Hauptströmung amerikanischer Architektur eindringen kann. Frank Gehry scheint dies auf seine persönliche Art und Weise mit seinen umfassenden Aufträgen für die Walt Disney Concert Hall in Los Angeles und dem American Center in Paris bereits erreicht zu haben. Das American Center – am rechten Ufer der Seine in der Nähe des neuen Finanzministeriums in Bercy

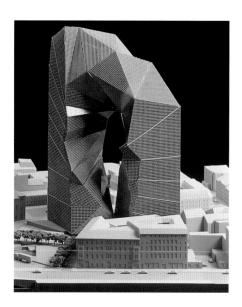

portantes pour le Walt Disney Concert Hall de Los Angeles ou l'American Center à Paris. Ce dernier projet, situé sur la rive droite de la Seine, proche du nouveau Ministère des Finances de Bercy et face au bâtiment de la Bibliothèque de France à été dessiné à partir de l'intérieur. La façade sur rue ne livre aucune clé sur l'usage inhabituel de l'espace que Gehry a inventé pour cette structure complexe. Du côté du parc et du fleuve, cependant, les façades extérieures créent des harmonies dynamiques. Plein d'humour et inattendu dans son utilisation des matériaux et des formes, il semble que Gehry ait aujourd'hui endossé le rôle de principal architecte américain.

Heureusement, ceci ne signifie pas que d'autres styles et d'autres tendances ne continueront pas à exister et à bien se porter. Avec moins d'opportunités de

Charles Moore: Piazza d'Italia, New
Orleans, Louisiana, 1977-78

structure. On the river and park side, however, the external façades create dynamic harmonies. Humorous and unexpected in his use of materials and forms, it is Frank Gehry who seems today to have taken on the role of the leading American architect.

This fortunately does not mean that other styles, and other trends will not continue to exist and flourish. With fewer opportunities to build than they may have had in the past, European architects do not seem today to exert the kind of large influence that they did in America in Colonial times, in the 19th century, or even when the masters of the Bauhaus found refuge in the United States. American architecture, nonetheless, open to a wide variety of influences, today seems to be more independent and perhaps more original than it was at most times in the past. This is where the trends of coming years will first be brought forth.

und genau gegenüber dem Gebäude der Bibliothèque de France gelegen – wurde von innen heraus entwickelt. Die Straßenfassade läßt keinerlei Schlüsse auf die ungewöhnliche Raumaufteilung zu, die Gehry für dieses komplexe Projekt entwickelte. Auf der zum Fluß und zum Park gewandten Seite dagegen erzeugen die Fassaden eine dynamische Harmonie. Durch seinen Humor und seine ungewöhnliche Verwendung von Materialien und Formen hat Frank Gehry heute allem Anschein nach die Rolle des führenden amerikanischen Architekten übernommen.

Dies bedeutet glücklicherweise nicht, daß andere Stilrichtungen und Strömungen nicht weiterhin existieren und gedeihen. Da die europäischen Architekten heutzutage nicht mehr in gleichem Maße wie früher bauen können, scheinen sie einen geringeren Einfluß auf Amerika auszuüben, als dies beispielsweise in der Kolonialzeit, im 19. Jahrhundert oder zu Zeiten des Bauhaus' in den Vereinigten Staaten der Fall war. Obwohl die amerikanische Architektur einer Vielzahl von Einflüssen gegenüber offen ist, erscheint sie heute unabhängiger und vielleicht origineller als je zuvor. Hier werden die Trends der kommenden Jahre entstehen.

construire que par le passé, les architectes européens ne paraissent plus en mesure d'exercer la puissante influence qui fut la leur à l'époque coloniale, au XIXème siècle, ou même lorsque les maîtres du Bauhaus trouvèrent refuge aux Etats-Unis. L'architecture américaine reste néanmoins toujours ouverte à de multiples influences et paraît aujourd'hui plus indépendante et peut-être plus originale que jamais au cours de son passé. C'est ici que naîtront les tendances de l'architecture pour les années à venir.

ARQUITECTONICA
PETER **EISENMAN**
FRANK O. **GEHRY**
CHARLES **GWATHMEY**
STEVEN **HOLL**
HELMUT **JAHN**
RICHARD **MEIER**
CHARLES **MOORE**
MORPHOSIS
ERIC OWEN **MOSS**
IEOH MING **PEI**
ANTOINE **PREDOCK**
BART **PRINCE**
SITE
ROBERT **VENTURI**

ARQUITECTONICA

Since its founding in 1977, the Arquitectonica group, headed by Bernardo Fort-Brescia (* 1951), and his wife Laurinda Hope Spear (* 1950) has occupied a special place in the list of contemporary architects. Based in Miami, but often taking advantage of the fact that Fort-Brescia was born in Lima, Peru, they have succeeded in completing an impressive series of large-scale projects. Often characterized by unusual forms or colors, well suited to the climate and style of Miami, their buildings are nonetheless situated in the mainstream of Neo-Modernist architecture. They offer an excitement within the limits of reason, which does not really challenge the basis of architecture, as might Frank Gehry, or, in a more intellectual style, Peter Eisenman. Their version of Modernism is not nostalgic, but rather young, like the principals, and turned toward the future.

Seit ihrer Gründung 1977 nimmt Arquitectonica, die von Bernardo Fort-Brescia (* 1951) und seiner Frau Laurinda Hope Spear (* 1950) geleitet wird, einen besonderen Platz innerhalb der zeitgenössischen Architektur ein. Die Gruppe hat ihren Sitz in Miami, macht es sich aber häufig zunutze, daß Fort-Brescia in Lima, Peru, geboren wurde. Dadurch hat sie eine beeindruckende Anzahl von Großprojekten dort fertiggestellt. Obwohl sich ihre Bauten oft durch ungewöhnliche Formen und Farben auszeichnen und Klima und Stil Miamis angepaßt sind, liegen sie dennoch im Trend neo-modernistischer Architektur. Arquitectonica erprobt innerhalb vernünftiger Grenzen Neues, das den Boden der Architektur aber nicht verläßt, wie es etwa Frank Gehry oder, auf einer eher intellektuellen Ebene, Peter Eisenman praktizieren. Ihre Auffassung der Moderne ist nicht nostalgisch, sondern ebenso jung und zukunftsorientiert wie sie selbst.

Depuis sa fondation (1977), le groupe Arquitectonica, dirigé par Bernardo Fort-Brescia (né en 1951) et sa femme, Laurinda Hope Spear (née en 1950) occupe une place à part dans l'architecture contemporaine. Basés à Miami, mais profitant souvent du fait que Fort-Brescia soit né à Lima, au Pérou, ils ont réussi à réaliser une impressionnante série d'importants projets. Leurs constructions se caractérisent souvent par des formes ou des couleurs inhabituelles, bien adaptées au climat et au style de Miami, mais ne s'en rattachent pas moins au courant néo-moderniste. Elles procurent un effet de surprise, dans des limites raisonnables, qui ne remet pas fondamentalement en question les bases de l'architecture, comme savent le faire Frank Gehry ou, dans un style plus intellectuel, Peter Eisenman. Cette version du Modernisme n'est pas nostalgique mais plutôt jeune, comme ses initiateurs d'ailleurs, et tournée vers l'avenir.

The Atlantis, Miami, Florida, 1980-82

There is a precarious element in all of our buildings.

Es liegt ein Moment der Unsicherheit in all unseren Bauten.

Dans toutes nos constructions, il existe un élément de précarité.

LAURINDA HOPE SPEAR

CENTER FOR INNOVATIVE TECHNOLOGY 1985-88
HERNDON, VIRGINIA

This office and research complex is located on a densely wooded hill. The most striking element is a tower whose dimensions increase as it rises. Although nature surrounds the building, there is no attempt to make it blend into the forest. The unusual angles and colorful cladding are typical of the architects, who have succeeded in giving this Center a feeling of movement appropriate to the idea of the up-to-date technology which is the theme of the project.

Der Büro- und Forschungskomplex liegt auf einem dicht bewaldeten Hügel. Sein auffallendstes Merkmal ist ein Turm, dessen Umfang mit steigender Höhe zunimmt. Obwohl das Gebäude von Wäldern umgeben ist, unternahm man keinen Versuch, es harmonisch darin einzufügen. Typisch für Arquitectonica sind ungewöhnliche Winkel und farbige Verkleidungen, die dem Gebäude einen Ausdruck von Bewegung verleihen, der dem Grundthema des Projekts entspricht – der Entwicklung innovativer Technik.

Cet ensemble conçu pour des bureaux et des laboratoires de recherche est situé sur une colline très boisée. L'élément le plus frappant est la tour dont la largeur augmente avec la hauteur. Bien que la nature entoure ce bâtiment, on n'a pas été tenté de le dissimuler dans la forêt. Les angles inhabituels et le revêtement coloré sont typiques d'Arquitectonica qui a réussi à animer ce centre de recherches d'un mouvement évocateur des technologies d'avant-garde qui sont sa raison d'être.

The CIT is a composition of unexpected angles, curves and colors. In contrast to the forest around the building, there is an ordered garden on the rooftop plaza over the parking area.

Das CIT bildet eine Synthese aus ungewöhnlichen Winkeln, Krümmungen und Farben. Im Kontrast zur bewaldeten Umgebung wurde auf der Dachfläche des Parkhauses ein geometrisch strukturierter Garten angelegt.

Le CIT est une composition d'angles, de courbes et de couleurs inattendus. Contrastant avec la forêt environnante, un jardin très dessiné a été créé sur la terrasse au-dessus du parking.

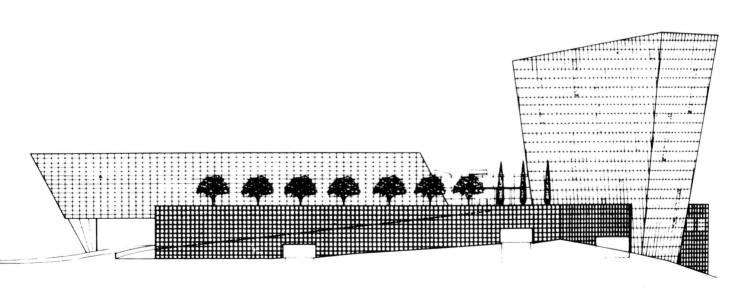

MULDER HOUSE 1983-85
LIMA, PERU

Set on a lot which is hardly wider than the building, the Mulder House demonstrates the ability of Arquitectonica to create unusual forms beginning with a very matter-of-fact floor plan divided into four functional zones. Despite the pink curves of the entrance, the basic structure is a simple two story rectangle, with intersecting walls which serve to define the volumes and unite the quadrants of the house. This house could just as easily have been built in Miami as in Lima.

Mit dem Mulder House – das auf einem Grundstück erbaut wurde, das nur wenig größer ist als das Gebäude selbst – demonstrierte Arquitectonica ihre Fähigkeit, ungewöhnliche Formen auf einem eher nüchternen Grundriß zu errichten, der hier in vier Funktionszonen eingeteilt ist. Trotz des pinkfarbenen geschwungenen Eingangs besteht die Grundform des Gebäudes aus einem einfachen zweigeschossigen Rechteck. Einander kreuzende Wände definieren den Baukörper und verbinden die vier Zonen des Hauses, das sowohl in Lima als auch in Miami stehen könnte.

Construite sur un terrain à peine plus large qu'elle, la Mulder House démontre l'habileté d'Arquitectonica à créer des formes inhabituelles en partant d'un plan très banal en quatre zones fonctionnelles. Malgré les courbes roses de l'entrée, la structure n'est à la base qu'un simple rectangle de deux étages, avec des murs qui s'entrecoupent, définissant les volumes et unifiant les quatre secteurs de cette maison qui pourrait aussi bien avoir été construite à Miami qu'à Lima.

A curved, pink volume, the entrance to the house, has an elliptical skylight to supplement the small windows. The notched, white wall is at the rear, and the red volumes are chimneys.

Der Eingang des Hauses besteht aus einem geschwungenen pinkfarbenen Baukörper, bei dem ein elliptisches Oberlicht die kleinen Fenster ergänzt. Die eingekerbte weiße Wand bildet die Rückfront; die roten Quader sind Kamine.

Volume rose et incurvé, l'entrée de la maison, dispose d'un lanterneau elliptique qui complète l'éclairage apporté par les petites fenêtres. Le mur blanc à encoches est l'arrière de la maison et les volumes rouges sont des cheminées.

Set against the Andes, the Banco de Crédito, is clad in black and white marble, steel, stucco, glass and pink slate. The elliptical glass-block lobby is a spectacular interior feature.

Vor dem Hintergrund der Anden liegt die Banco de Crédito mit ihren Verkleidungen aus schwarzem und weißem Marmor, Stahl, Stuck, Glas und rosa Schiefer. Im Inneren des Gebäudes bildet die ellipsenförmige Lobby aus Glasbausteinen einen spektakulären Blickfang.

Situé face aux Andes, le Banco de Crédito est recouvert de marbre noir et blanc, d'acier, de stuc, de verre et d'ardoises roses. Le hall elliptique, tout en verre, est très spectaculaire.

BANCO DE CRÉDITO 1983-88
LIMA, PERU

This headquarters building for the largest private bank in Peru is one of Arquitectonica's most powerful projects. The 50,000 square meter structure is situated in the La Molina suburban area, above the Peruvian capital, and manages to combine an impression of solidity with unexpected forms and colors. Despite the unusual appearance of the bank, the basic floor plan, arranged around an essentially square courtyard, is quite simple.

Die Zentrale der größten Privatbank Perus zählt zu den kraftvollsten Projekten der Gruppe Arquitectonica. Das Gebäude mit 50 000 m² liegt im Vorort La Molina, oberhalb des Stadtzentrums, und es verbindet ungewöhnliche Formen und Farben mit einem Eindruck von Solidität. Trotz des überraschenden Äußeren der Bank ist der eigentliche Grundriß – bei dem die Baukörper um einen quadratischen Innenhof angeordnet wurden – eher schlicht.

Le siège social de la plus importante banque privée du Pérou est l'un des projets les plus spectaculaires réalisés par Arquitectonica. Cette construction de 50 000 mètres carrés est implantée dans la banlieue de La Molina, au-dessus de la capitale péruvienne, et réussit à associer une impression de solidité à des formes et à des couleurs surprenantes. Si l'apparence est inusitée pour une banque, le plan des différents niveaux, organisé autour d'un espace carré, reste assez simple.

PETER **EISENMAN**

Peter Eisenman (* 1932) is one of the most controversial architects of his generation. A member of the »New York Five« group, he has spent more time teaching and writing than he has building. It was only recently, with his Wexner Center for the Visual Arts (Ohio State University, Columbus, Ohio, 1982-89) that he affirmed the need to give his ideas tangible form. Proceeding from an intellectual basis, influenced by French philosophers such as Jacques Derrida, he has used scientific concepts like plate tectonics, or the »weak forces« of nuclear physics to attempt a challenge to the very conception of the built environment. Although Modernist gridding sometimes appears in Eisenman's projects, there is a radical shifting of elements, which seems to be typical of the Deconstructivist movement, of which he is one of the leading lights.

Peter Eisenman (* 1932) ist einer der umstrittensten Architekten seiner Generation. Als Mitglied der »New York Five« widmete er dem Leben und Schreiben mehr Zeit als seiner eigenen Bautätigkeit. Erst mit dem Wexner Center for the Visual Arts (Ohio State University, Columbus, Ohio, 1982-89) kam er dem Wunsch nach, seine Ideen in greifbare Formen umzusetzen. Ausgehend von einer intellektuellen Ebene und beeinflußt von französischen Philosophen wie Jacques Derrida, arbeitet er mit wissenschaftlichen Konzepten wie der Plattentektonik oder den »schwachen Wechselkräften« der Atomphysik als Versuch, das Konzept der baulichen Umgebung herauszufordern. Obwohl in Eisenmans Projekten vereinzelt modernistisches Gitterwerk zu finden ist, fällt bei ihm vor allem die für den Dekonstruktivismus typische radikale Verschiebung der Baukörper auf. Dies macht ihn zu einem der führenden Köpfe dieses Trends.

Peter Eisenman (né en 1932) est l'un des architectes les plus controversés de sa génération. Membre du groupe des «New York Five», il a consacré plus de temps à enseigner et à écrire qu'à construire. Ce n'est que récemment, avec le Wexner Center for the Visual Arts (Ohio State University, Columbus, Ohio, 1982-89) qu'il a affirmé le besoin de donner à ses idées une forme tangible. A partir d'une base intellectuelle, influencée par la philosophie française (Jacques Derrida), il a utilisé des concepts scientifiques comme la tectonique des plaques ou les «forces faibles» de la physique nucléaire pour tenter de lancer un défi à la conception même du construit. Bien que la trame moderniste apparaisse parfois dans ses projets, on y trouve un décalage radical des éléments qui semble typique du mouvement déconstructiviste dont il est une des principales figures.

Wexner Center for the Visual Arts, Columbus, Ohio, 1982-89

Architecture only exists as it displaces itself.

Architektur existiert nur dann, wenn sie sich selbst verdrängt.

L'architecture n'existe que lorsqu'elle réussit à être déplacée.

PETER EISENMAN

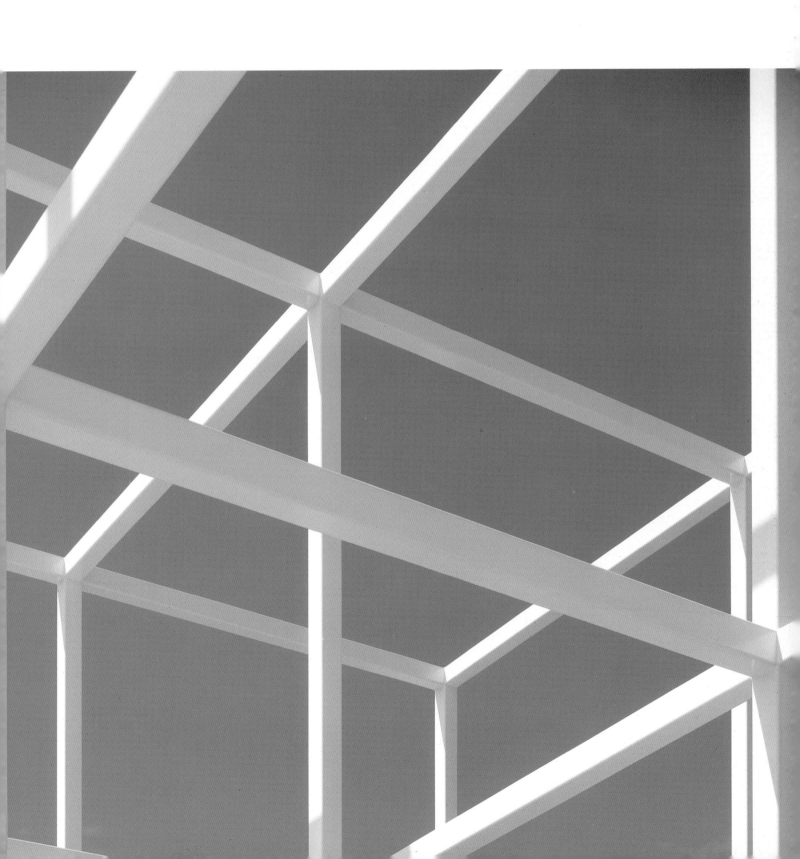

WEXNER CENTER FOR THE VISUAL ARTS 1982-89
OHIO STATE UNIVERSITY, COLUMBUS, OHIO

Inserted into a cleft between existing structures at Ohio State University, the Wexner Center remains Peter Eisenman's most significant built work. Although unconventional in form, the building which contains art galleries, theaters, a laboratory and a fine arts library, is to function in a relatively traditional way. Though opposed to historicism as a style, Eisenman marked the building with fragmentary brick towers which recall the armory standing on the site until 1958.

Eingefügt in eine Baulücke zwischen bereits existierenden Gebäuden der Ohio State University ist das Wexner Center Peter Eisenmans bedeutendstes Bauwerk. Trotz seiner unkonventionellen Form soll das Gebäude eher traditionelle Aufgaben erfüllen: es beherbergt Kunstgalerien und Theater, ein Labor sowie eine Kunstbibliothek. Obwohl Eisenman den Historismus als Stil ablehnt, versah er das Gebäude mit fragmentarischen Türmen aus Ziegelsteinen, die an das Zeughaus erinnern, das bis 1958 an dieser Stelle gestanden hatte.

Inséré entre deux bâtiments pré-existants de l'Ohio State University, le Wexner Center reste l'œuvre construite la plus significative d'Eisenman. Bien que de forme non conventionnelle, l'édifice qui contient des galeries d'exposition, des salles de spectacle, un laboratoire et une bibliothèque artistique, est conçu pour fonctionner de façon relativement classique. Même s'il est opposé à l'historicisme en tant que style, Eisenman a marqué son bâtiment d'ébauches de tours de briques rappelant le dépôt d'armes qui se trouvait sur le site jusqu'en 1958.

The two-story lobby (left) shares a sense of displaced volumes and structural surprises with the exterior. An aerial view shows the insertion of the Center between existing structures.

Die zweigeschossige Lobby (links) vermittelt wie die Fassade den Eindruck verschobener Quader und architektonischer Überraschungen. Ein Luftbild zeigt die Einordnung des Centers zwischen die bestehenden Gebäude.

Haut de deux étages, le hall (à gauche), comme l'extérieur, donne au visiteur une certaine sensation de glissements de volumes et de surprises structurelles. Une vue aérienne montre l'insertion du Centre entre les structures pré-existantes.

GREATER COLUMBUS
CONVENTION CENTER 1989-93
COLUMBUS, OHIO

Peter Eisenman's largest commission to date, with a floor area over 50,000 square meters, the Columbus Convention Center represents an effort to »create a new type of public architecture«. Clad in metal siding, the building twists and turns toward North High Street, where abruptly angled façades are intended to give an impression of »movement and dynamism«. The architect admits that a number of the interior spaces of the Center were redesigned because the client considered them too radical.

Das Columbus Convention Center mit seiner Grundfläche von über 50 000 m² ist bis heute Peter Eisenmans größter Auftrag und repräsentiert den Versuch, »einen neuen Typ von Architektur für die Öffentlichkeit zu entwickeln«. Das mit Metallplatten verkleidete Gebäude, dessen vor- und rückspringende Fassaden einen Eindruck von »Bewegung und Dynamik« vermitteln sollen, erstreckt sich in Windungen und Krümmungen entlang der North High Street. Der Architekt räumt ein, daß verschiedene Innenräume noch einmal überarbeitet wurden, da der Auftraggeber sie als zu radikal empfand.

La plus importante commande jamais reçue par Eisenman, le Columbus Convention Center (plus de 50 000 mètres carrés au sol) est une tentative de «créer un nouveau type d'architecture publique». Recouvert de métal, le bâtiment se tord littéralement pour se tourner vers North High Street, où des façades coupées à angles vifs donnent une impression de «mouvement et de dynamisme». L'architecte a admis que certains espaces intérieurs du Centre avaient été redessinés car le client les trouvait trop radicaux.

Located on the former site of Union Station, the Center is at the northern end of downtown Columbus. Its forms are related to the architect's study of scientific or geological concepts.

Das Columbus Convention Center liegt an der Stelle der früheren Union Station am Nordrand der Innenstadt von Columbus. Seine Formen stehen im Zusammenhang mit Eisenmans Untersuchungen wissenschaftlicher wie geologischer Konzepte.

Construit sur une ancienne gare, le Centre se trouve à l'extrémité nord du centre ville de Columbus. Ses formes rappellent des concepts scientifiques, en particulier géologiques, familiers à l'architecte.

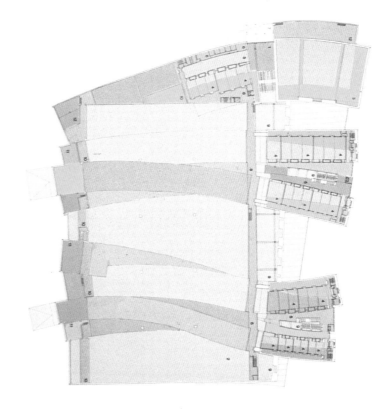

FRANK O. **GEHRY**

Frank O. Gehry (* 1929) may be the most influential architect working in the world today. Not only has he successfully called into question the forms which modern architecture has taken for granted, but he has done the same for materials of construction. It is not that steel and concrete are absent from his work, but rather that chain link, corrugated aluminum, or utility grade construction board are present. Gehry seems to be as much at ease building a giant fish (Fish Dance Restaurant, Kobe, Japan, 1984), as he is with an office building whose façade is dominated by a huge pair of binoculars (designed by Claes Oldenburg for Chiat/Day, Venice, California, 1989). In a way, Gehry is at times closer to contemporary sculpture than to architecture, but no matter how unexpected the external forms, the interiors of his buildings remain extremely viable.

Frank O. Gehry (* 1929) ist heute der vielleicht einflußreichste Architekt der Welt. Er stellte nicht nur die Formen, sondern auch die Baumaterialien in Frage, die die moderne Architektur als selbstverständlich akzeptiert hatte. Gehry baut zwar nicht ohne Stahl und Beton, er verwendet aber auch Kettenglieder, Wellblech und Fertigbauteile. Darüber hinaus scheint Gehry ein ebenso großes Vergnügen daran zu haben, einen gigantischen Fisch zu bauen (Fish Dance Restaurant, Kobe, Japan, 1984) wie die Fassade eines Verwaltungsgebäudes mit einem riesigen Fernglas zu krönen (entworfen von Claes Oldenburg für Chiat/Day, Venice, California, 1989). Manchmal sind Gehrys Arbeiten der modernen Bildhauerei näher als der Architektur, aber trotz verblüffendem Aussehen ist das Innere seiner Gebäude immer funktionell.

Frank O. Gehry (né en 1929) est peut-être l'architecte le plus influent actuellement à l'œuvre dans le monde. Non seulement il a remis en question avec succès des formes que l'architecture moderne tenait pour établies, mais il a agi de même avec les matériaux de construction. Ce n'est pas que l'acier et le béton soient absents de ses œuvres, mais il se plaît plutôt à utiliser le treillage métallique, la tôle ondulée d'aluminium ou des planches de bois brut. Gehry semble être aussi à l'aise dans la construction d'un poisson géant (Fish Dance Restaurant, Kobe, Japon, 1984) que dans celle d'un immeuble de bureaux dont la façade est dominée par une énorme paire de jumelles (dessinée par Claes Oldenburg pour Chiat/Day, Venice, Californie, 1989). En ce sens, Gehry est parfois plus proche de la sculpture contemporaine que de l'architecture, mais aussi inattendues ses formes extérieures puissent-elles être, l'intérieur de ces bâtiments reste extrêmement vivable.

University of Toledo Art Building, Toledo, Ohio, 1990-92

By definition, a building is a sculpture, because it is a three-dimensional object.

Ein Gebäude ist per definitionem eine Skulptur, da es ein dreidimensionales Objekt darstellt.

Par définition, un bâtiment est une sculpture, puisque c'est un objet en trois dimensions.

FRANK O. GEHRY

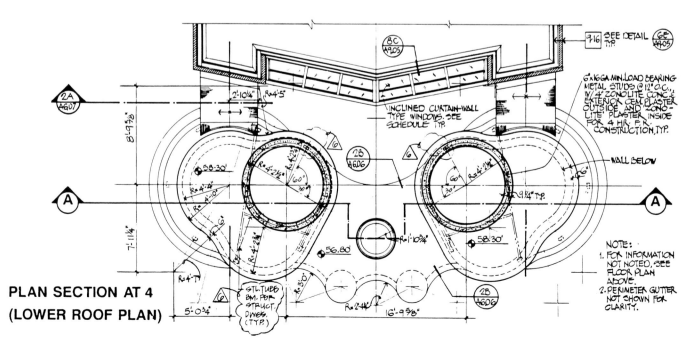

**PLAN SECTION AT 4
(LOWER ROOF PLAN)**

NOTE:
1. FOR INFORMATION NOT NOTED, SEE FLOOR PLAN ABOVE.
2. PERIMETER GUTTER NOT SHOWN FOR CLARITY.

INCLINED CURTAIN-WALL TYPE WINDOWS. SEE SCHEDULE TYP.

6"x16 GA. MIN. LOAD BEARING METAL STUDS @ 12" O.C., W/ 4" ZONOLITE CONC. & EXTERIOR CEM. PLASTER OUTSIDE, AND 'ZONO-LITE' PLASTER INSIDE FOR 4 HR. F.R. CONSTRUCTION, TYP.

WALL BELOW

STL. TUBE BM. PER STRUCT. DWGS. (TYP.)

CHIAT/DAY MAIN STREET 1984-91
VENICE, CALIFORNIA

Located four blocks from the Pacific, this three-story building for an advertising agency is on an L-shaped site which was subjected to rigorous local zoning restrictions. Its most surprising feature is the enormous pair of binoculars which serves as the entrance to an underground parking lot for three hundred cars.

Dieses dreigeschossige Gebäude einer Werbeagentur liegt vier Blocks vom Pazifik entfernt. Es wurde auf einem L-förmigen Grundstück errichtet, das strengen örtlichen Baubestimmungen unterlag. Ein enormes Fernglas, das als Eingang zu einem unterirdischen Parkhaus für 300 Autos dient, bildet einen besonders überraschenden Blickfang.

Situé à quatre pâtés de maisons du Pacifique, ce bâtiment de trois étages réalisé pour une agence de publicité est implanté sur un terrain en L soumis à une réglementation d'urbanisme particulièrement rigoureuse. Sa caractéristique la plus surprenante est certainement l'énorme paire de jumelles qui sert d'entrée à un parking souterrain de trois cents places.

Conceived in collaboration with the sculptors Claes Oldenburg and Coosje van Bruggen, the binoculars are part of the building, containing conference or research space.

Das Fernglas wurde in Zusammenarbeit mit den Bildhauern Claes Oldenburg und Coosje van Bruggen entworfen und ist Teil des Gebäudes mit Konferenzsälen und Arbeitsräumen.

Conçues en collaboration avec les sculpteurs Claes Oldenburg et Coosje van Bruggen, ces jumelles font partie de l'édifice et contiennent d'ailleurs un espace de réunion ou de travail.

The pavilion to the left, in the lake, is above the master bedroom. To the right, two views of the double-height living room. A section and floor plan reveal the full complexity of the design.

Der in den See hineinragende Pavillon (links) liegt oberhalb des Hauptschlafraums. Rechts davon zwei Ansichten des Wohnzimmers, das sich über zwei Etagen erstreckt. Ein Schnitt und der Grundriß verdeutlichen die Komplexität des Entwurfs.

Le toit-pavillon de gauche, est situé au-dessus de la chambre principale elle-même construite dans le «lac». A droite, deux vues du living-room à double-hauteur. Le plan masse et l'élévation révèlent la réelle complexité du dessin.

SCHNABEL RESIDENCE 1986-89
BRENTWOOD, CALIFORNIA

This particularly complex house of about 550 square meters, is clad in stucco, copper, and lead-coated copper. A lap pool on one side, and a shallow »lake« on another, give an impression that the house is intimately related to water. As is often the case in Gehry's California buildings, some of the forms serve to shield the residents from the sun.

Dieses Haus von etwa 550 m² ist mit Stuck, Kupferplatten und verzinktem Kupfer verkleidet. Ein langgestrecktes Schwimmbecken auf der einen und ein flacher Teich auf der anderen Seite zeugen von der engen Verbundenheit des Hauses mit dem Wasser. Wie in vielen seiner kalifornischen Projekte dient ein Teil dieser Formen als Sonnenschutz für die Bewohner.

Cette maison particulièrement complexe de 550 mètres carrés environ est recouverte de stuc, de cuivre apparent ou sous plomb. Un bassin d'un côté, et un «lac» en creux d'un autre, créent un rapport intime entre l'eau et la maison. Comme c'est souvent le cas dans les œuvres californiennes de Gehry, certaines formes servent tout simplement à abriter du soleil.

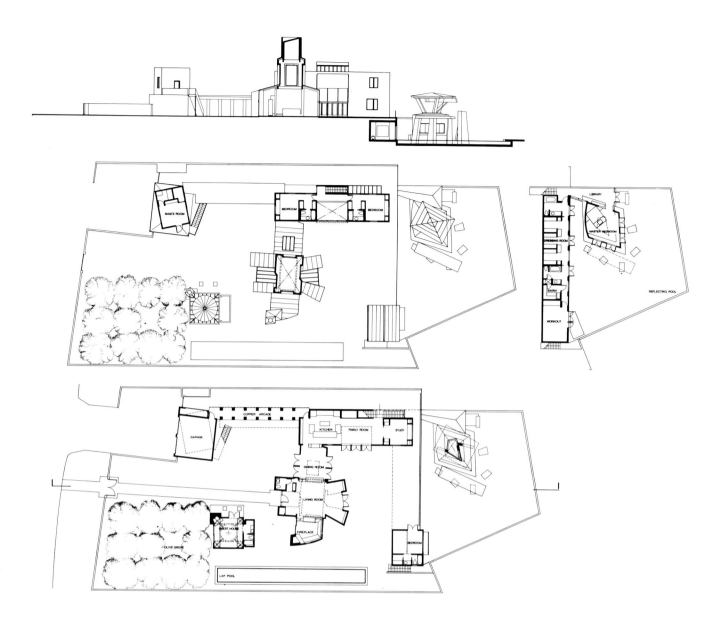

Views of opposite sides of the building show the opaque metallic façade as opposed to the glass walls facing large trees. Gehry's free-flowing drawing (right page) gives a sense of his creative drive.

Ansichten der verschiedenen Seiten des Gebäudes zeigen dessen undurchsichtige Metallfassade im Gegensatz zu den großen Glaswänden mit den davorstehenden Bäumen. Gehrys freie Zeichnung (rechte Seite) vermittelt einen Eindruck seiner Kreativität.

Les vues des deux côtés du bâtiment montrent la façade métallique opaque opposée aux murs de verre qui donnent sur les grands arbres. Le dessin très libre de Gehry traduit bien son inspiration créative.

UNIVERSITY OF TOLEDO ART BUILDING 1990-92
TOLEDO, OHIO

Like the structure Gehry designed for the Guggenheim in Bilbao (not yet built), the University of Toledo Art Building has one façade which brings to mind a fortress, clad in lead-coated copper. This impression is reinforced by the grass-covered berm which rises to its base. In this case, the architect intended to create a contrast with the adjacent neoclassical, white marble-clad Toledo Museum of Art. Other surfaces are covered with glass, permitting ample daylight to enter the building.

Ähnlich wie bei Gehrys Entwurf für das Guggenheim Museum in Bilbao (noch nicht gebaut) besitzt das University of Toledo Art Building eine mit verzinkten Kupferplatten verkleidete Fassade, die an eine Festung erinnert. Dieser Eindruck wird durch den grasbewachsenen Wall unterstrichen, der zum Fundament hin ansteigt. In diesem Fall zielt der Architekt darauf ab, einen Kontrast zur weißen Marmorverkleidung des angrenzenden neoklassizistischen Toledo Museum of Art zu schaffen. Die anderen Oberflächen bestehen aus Glas, so daß genügend Tageslicht in das Gebäude einfällt.

Comme l'édifice conçu par Gehry pour le Guggenheim Museum à Bilbao (non encore construit), ce bâtiment présente une façade recouverte de cuivre enduit de plomb qui évoque une forteresse. Cette impression est renforcée par la berme gazonnée qui monte jusqu'à sa base. L'architecte voulait créer un contraste avec le Toledo Museum of Art en marbre blanc et d'esprit néoclassique tout proche. D'autres surfaces sont recouvertes de verre pour permettre à la lumière du jour d'inonder l'intérieur du bâtiment.

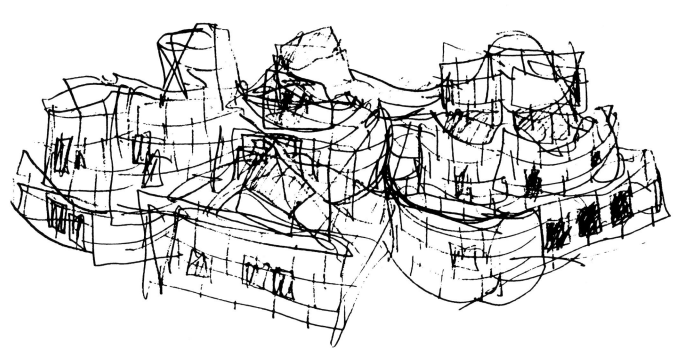

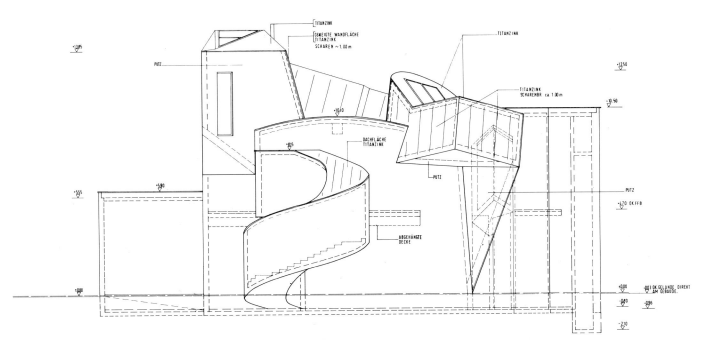

SÜDOSTANSICHT   M.1:50

VITRA INTERNATIONAL FURNITURE MANUFACTURING FACILITY AND MUSEUM 1989
WEIL AM RHEIN, GERMANY

The twisting volumes of this building, and others in a similar style by Frank Gehry can be linked not only to Russian Constructivism, but also to German Expressionism. Its interior has been compared to Kurt Schwitters' Merzbau (Hanover). Gehry himself speaks of »frozen motion«. The complex includes a chair-assembly plant and offices as well as the museum. A large Claes Oldenburg sculpture of tools in front seems a natural complement to the architecture.

Ähnlich wie bei anderen Bauten von Frank Gehry stehen auch die dynamischen Baukörper dieses Gebäudes nicht nur mit den russischen Konstruktivisten, sondern auch mit dem deutschen Expressionismus in Beziehung. Das Innere ist mit Kurt Schwitters' Merzbau (Hannover) verglichen worden; Gehry selbst spricht bei seiner Beschreibung des Vitra-Museums von »erstarrter Bewegung«. Zum Komplex gehören neben einer Stuhlfabrik auch Büroräume und ein Museum. Eine große Werkzeug-Skulptur von Claes Oldenburg vor dem Gebäude stellt eine natürliche Ergänzung dar.

Les volumes torturés de ce bâtiment, ainsi que d'autres construits dans un style similaire par Frank Gehry, peuvent être rapprochés non seulement de certains constructivistes russes mais aussi de l'expressionnisme allemand. Son intérieur a été comparé au Merzbau de Kurt Schwitters (Hanovre). Gehry lui-même parle de «mouvement gelé» pour décrire le musée Vitra. L'ensemble comprend une chaîne de montage de sièges, des bureaux et un musée. Une grande sculpture de Claes Oldenburg représentant des outils semble compléter tout naturellement la composition architecturale.

The »frozen motion« sought by Gehry lends itself to the unexpected succession of interior spaces. Skylights, shaped to bounce and diffuse the light, bring daylight to the galleries.

Die von Gehry angestrebte »erstarrte Bewegung« führt zu einer Reihe ungewöhnlicher Innenräume. Oberlichter, die das Licht sowohl zentrieren als auch zerstreuen, verteilen Tageslicht über die Galerien.

Le «mouvement gelé» recherché par Gehry se prête à une succession inattendue d'espaces intérieurs. Les verrières, conçues pour refléter et diffuser la lumière, introduisent la lumière du jour dans les galeries.

FESTIVAL DISNEY 1992
EURO DISNEY, MARNE-LA-VALLÉE, FRANCE

Gehry says that the metal-clad towers of this complex, which are linked by a delicate web of tiny lights came to his mind when he imagined the electrical relays often seen near railroad stations. The freely shaped buildings were added afterwards. Of the architects who participated in Euro Disney, Gehry is exceptional in that he was given a free hand to design. He has expressed regret that he allowed Disney to design the signs for the restaurants and shops.

Die Idee zu den metallverkleideten Türmen, die untereinander mit einem feinen Gewebe aus kleinen Lampen verbunden sind, entwickelte Gehry bei der Betrachtung elektrischer Relais in der Nähe von Bahnhöfen. Die frei gestalteten Gebäude wurden später hinzugefügt. Von den an Euro Disney beteiligten Architekten hatte Gehry als einziger freie Hand bei seinen Entwürfen. Heute bedauert er nur, daß er Disney die Gestaltung der Schilder für Restaurants und Läden überließ.

Gehry a déclaré que ses tours recouvertes de métal et reliées par un faisceau de petites lumières lui furent inspirées par les relais électriques que l'on trouve dans les gares. Les bâtiments aux formes très libres furent conçus dans un second temps. De tous les architectes qui participèrent à la construction d'Euro Disney, Gehry est le seul à avoir bénéficié d'une liberté totale. Il a regretté d'avoir permis à Disney de dessiner les enseignes des restaurants et des boutiques.

The views and sections give a partial idea of the buildings in the Festival Disney complex. The colored, stainless steel-clad towers, which unite the structures, are visible here.

Die Ansichten und Schnitte geben einen ungefähren Eindruck von den Gebäuden des Festival Disney Komplex. Die farbig verkleideten Türme aus rostfreiem Edelstahl lassen eine optische Verbindung der einzelnen Baukörper entstehen.

Ces photos et ce plan de coupe donnent une idée partielle de la place des bâtiments dans le complexe «Festival Disney». On peut voir les tours d'acier inoxydable colorées qui donnent une unité à l'ensemble.

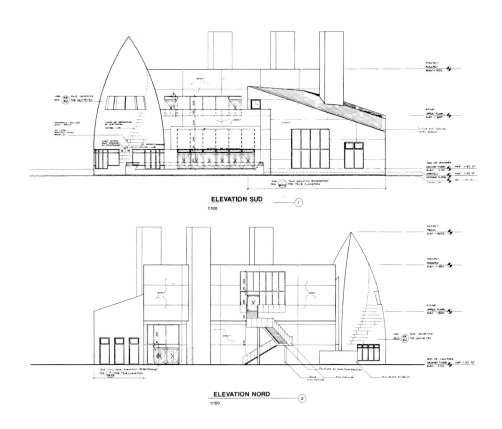

ELEVATION SUD
1:100

ELEVATION NORD
1:100

CHARLES **GWATHMEY**

A member of the »New York Five«, Charles Gwathmey (* 1938) has been more faithful to the inspiration of Le Corbusier than some other members of the group. Many of his buildings can be understood as a rotation of the vocabulary of Modernism through space. This sort of exploration of formal possibilities has also fascinated John Hejduk, but Gwathmey remains a more active builder. His continuing use of a Modernist vocabulary, for example, in the De Menil House (Long Island, 1984) is proof of the movement's enduring vitality. Charles Gwathmey is responsible for one of the most visible recent New York buildings – his controversial addition to Frank Lloyd Wright's Guggenheim Museum (1992). Although Gwathmey added a rectangular block, with bunker-like slits to the existing building, he also lovingly restored the curves of Wright's 1959 masterpiece.

Als Mitglied der »New York Five« folgte Charles Gwathmey (* 1938) den Ideen Le Corbusiers treuer als jeder andere der Gruppe. Viele seiner Bauten können als Rotation des Vokabulars der Moderne durch den Raum verstanden werden. Diese Art der Erforschung formaler Möglichkeiten faszinierte auch John Hejduk, wobei Gwathmey jedoch der aktivere Baumeister blieb. Sein fortgesetzter Gebrauch von Formen der Moderne, wie z. B. im De Menil House (Long Island, 1984), zeigt die kontinuierliche Vitalität dieser Bewegung. Charles Gwathmey zeichnet verantwortlich für eines der herausragendsten New Yorker Gebäude, den umstrittenen Anbau an Frank Lloyd Wrights Guggenheim Museum (1992). Obwohl Gwathmey an den bereits bestehenden Bau einen rechtwinkligen Block mit bunkerähnlichen Öffnungen anfügte, restaurierte er dennoch einfühlsam die gerundeten Formen an Wrights Meisterwerk aus dem Jahr 1959.

Membre des «New York Five», Charles Gwathmey (né en 1938) s'est montré plus fidèle à l'inspiration de Le Corbusier que d'autres membres du groupe. Nombre de ses édifices peuvent s'expliquer par une rotation dans l'espace d'éléments de nature moderniste. Ce type d'exploration des possibilités formelles a également fasciné John Hejduk, mais Gwathmey a construit davantage. Son recours permanent au vocabulaire moderniste, par exemple pour la De Menil House (Long Island, 1984), est la preuve de la continuité de la vitalité de ce mouvement. Charles Gwathmey est responsable de l'un des immeubles les plus visibles et les plus controversés de New York: l'extension du Guggenheim Museum de Frank Lloyd Wright (1992). Bien qu'il ait ajouté un bloc parallélépipédique à ouvertures en meurtrières au bâtiment existant, il a également restauré avec beaucoup de soins les courbes du chef-d'œuvre qu'édifia Wright en 1959.

Architecture is not static, nor is perception.

Architektur ist ebensowenig statisch wie unsere Wahrnehmung.

L'architecture n'est pas statique. Ni la perception d'ailleurs.

CHARLES GWATHMEY

SOLOMON R. GUGGENHEIM
MUSEUM ADDITION 1982-92
NEW YORK, NEW YORK

The decision to add space to Frank
Lloyd Wright's 1959 masterpiece was
highly controversial, and the project of
Gwathmey/Siegel had to be revised as
a result of criticism. They are responsible, not only for the rectangular block
which stands behind the curvilinear
museum, but also for a spectacular
restoration of the original building, in
particular its rotunda and skylight
dome. Gwathmey's addition is responsible and modest, but certainly more
Modernist than Wright would have
wished.

Die Entscheidung für einen Erweiterungsbau zu Frank Lloyd Wrights Meisterwerk von 1959 war heftig umstrit-
ten, und das Projekt von Gwathmey/
Siegel mußte aufgrund der Kritiken
überarbeitet werden. Sie zeichnen
nicht nur für den viereckigen Block hin-
ter dem runden Museum verantwortlich, sondern auch für die spektakuläre
Restaurierung des Hauptgebäudes, besonders für die Rotunde und die Ober-
lichtkuppel. Gwathmeys Erweiterungsbau ist verantwortungsbewußt und gemäßigt, aber sicherlich moderner, als
Wright es sich gewünscht hätte.

La décision d'agrandir le chef-d'œuvre
de Frank Lloyd Wright (1959) a soule-
vé une immense controverse et le projet Gwathmey/Siegel dut être révisé
sous l'assaut des critiques. Tous deux
sont responsables non seulement de
l'immeuble parallélépipédique qui se
dresse derrière le musée curviligne,
mais également de la restauration
spectaculaire de celui-ci, en particulier
de la rotonde et de la verrière du dôme. L'extension de Gwathmey est sen-
sée et modeste, mais certainement
plus moderniste d'esprit que ne l'aurait souhaité Wright.

Left page: Taken at sunset. The addition,
with its bunker-like slits stands in stark contrast to Wright's curves. Under the restored
skylight is a work of the artist Dan Flavin,
exhibited at the opening in 1992.

Linke Seite: Bei Sonnenuntergang. Die bun-
kerartigen Fensterschlitze des Erweite-
rungsbaus stehen in starkem Kontrast zu
Wrights gerundete Formen. Unter dem re-
staurierten Oberlicht ist eine Arbeit des
Künstlers Dan Flavin zu sehen, die zur Eröff-
nung 1992 ausgestellt wurde.

Page de gauche: coucher du soleil. Avec
ses fenêtres évoquant un bunker, elle contraste fortement avec les courbes
wrightiennes. En bas, la verrière restaurée
et une œuvre de Dan Flavin, exposée lors
de la réouverture en 1992.

DISNEY'S CONTEMPORARY RESORT 1991
WALT DISNEY WORLD, LAKE BUENA VISTA, FLORIDA

The strong horizontal silhouette and the colors are intended to mark the structure, which includes a total of about 14,000 square meters, with a large entrance plaza.

Die betont horizontale Silhouette und die kräftigen Farben sind charakteristisch für einen Komplex, der inklusive einer großen Vorhalle 14 000 m² umfaßt.

La solide silhouette horizontale et les couleurs fortes signalent de loin l'édifice, qui compte environ 14 000 mètres carrés et une vaste place devant l'entrée.

This project is an extension to the Contemporary Hotel (1971) by Welton Becket. The most significant space is a 4000 square meter ballroom, intended to serve 3000 people. The architect's description is eloquent: »It is a building about expectation, aspiration, illusion and memory, that establishes a new sense of place and a dynamic though sympathetic extension of the original iconographic Hotel.« This is one of many recent examples in which Disney has called on reputed architects.

Bei diesem Projekt handelt es sich um einen Anbau an das Contemporary Hotel (1971) von Welton Becket. Der auffälligste Raum ist ein 4000 m² großer Ballsaal für 3000 Menschen. Die Beschreibung des Architekten spricht für sich: »Dieses Gebäude weckt Erwartungen und Sehnsüchte, Illusionen und Erinnerungen. Es begründet eine neue Raumauffassung und bildet eine dynamische und doch angepaßte Erweiterung des bestehenden ikonographischen Hotels.« Dieser Anbau ist eines von vielen Projekten der letzten Jahre, für das Disney bekannte Architekten gewinnen konnte.

Ce projet est une extension du Contemporary Hotel de Welton Becket (1971). L'espace le plus frappant est une salle de bal de 4000 mètres carrés destinée à accueillir 3000 personnes. La description de l'architecte est éloquente: «C'est un bâtiment sur le thème de l'attente, de l'aspiration, de l'illusion et de la mémoire qui crée un nouveau sens du lieu et une extension dynamique, mais en sympathie avec l'hôtel original.» C'est un des nombreux exemples récents de la volonté de Disney de faire appel à des architectes réputés.

1   EAST ELEVATION OF CONVENTION CENTER

2   SOUTH ELEVATION OF CONVENTION CENTER

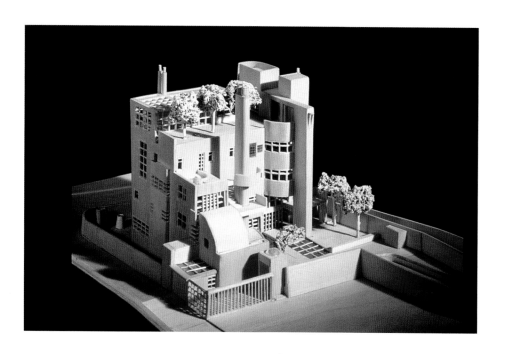

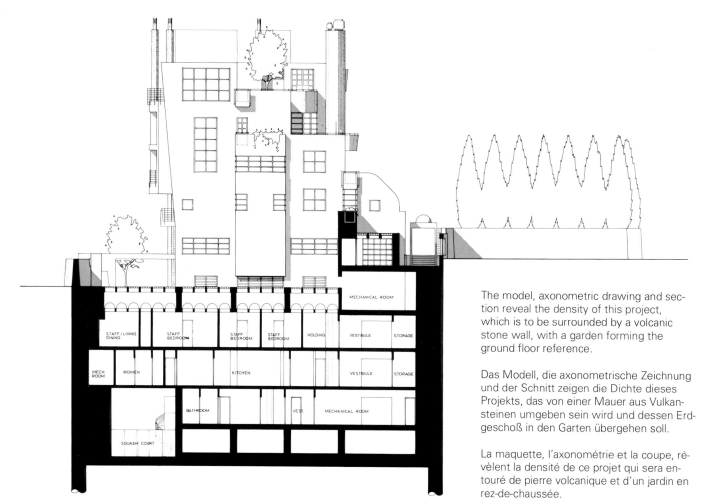

The model, axonometric drawing and section reveal the density of this project, which is to be surrounded by a volcanic stone wall, with a garden forming the ground floor reference.

Das Modell, die axonometrische Zeichnung und der Schnitt zeigen die Dichte dieses Projekts, das von einer Mauer aus Vulkansteinen umgeben sein wird und dessen Erdgeschoß in den Garten übergehen soll.

La maquette, l'axonométrie et la coupe, révèlent la densité de ce projet qui sera entouré de pierre volcanique et d'un jardin en rez-de-chaussée.

CHEN RESIDENCE, THE CHIMERE (PROJECT)

TAIPEI, TAIWAN

This residence is to be located on a 1000 square meter suburban site, and is divided into three areas for the family, service and entertainment. Because of the small lot, and the complex program, the house is dense, extending to four floors above the garden, and two basement levels. The architect indicates that the house provides a »summary of modern architectural principles«, and it does sum up many of his investigations into the formal possibilities provided by the Modernist vocabulary.

Das Wohnhaus soll auf einem 1000 m² großen Vorortgrundstück entstehen und ist in drei Bereiche aufgeteilt – Familie, Personal und Freizeit. Wegen des kleinen Grundstücks und des komplexen Entwurfs wirkt das Haus sehr kompakt: Es erstreckt sich über vier Stockwerke oberhalb des Gartens sowie zwei Untergeschosse. Der Architekt weist darauf hin, daß das Haus eine »Zusammenfassung moderner Architekturprinzipien« darstellt und viele seiner Gedanken über die formalen Möglichkeiten der Moderne darin enthalten sind.

Cette résidence, qui sera construite sur un terrain de 1000 mètres carrés en banlieue, est divisée en trois zones: famille, service et loisirs. Pour répondre à la complexité du programme et à la petite taille du terrain, la maison s'élève sur quatre niveaux au-dessus du jardin et deux niveaux de sous-sol. Pour l'architecte, elle offrira «un résumé des principes de l'architecture moderne». Elle illustre un certain nombre de ses recherches sur les possibilités formelles du vocabulaire moderniste.

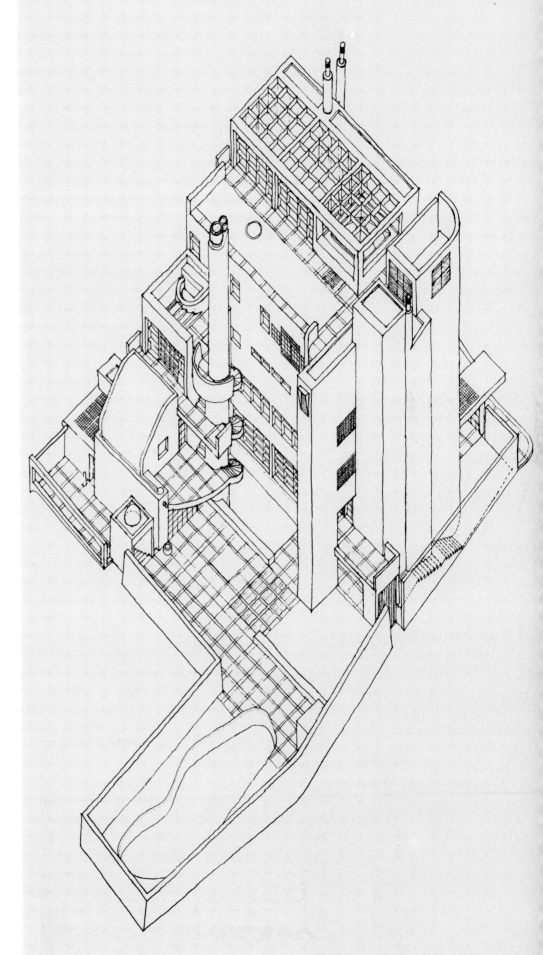

STEVEN HOLL

Steven Holl (* 1947) has declared that he is searching for »the elusive essence of architecture«. The Japanese architect Toyo Ito called Holl's buildings »more aural than visual«. This idea may be confirmed by the architect's own description of his Stretto House (Dallas, Texas, 1989-92), in which he draws a parallel between the house and Bartók's »Music for Strings, Percussion and Celeste«. There is a subtle, abstract rhythm in Steven Holl's work which distinguishes it ultimately from that of Le Corbusier, who undoubtedly remains the main influence on him. Another interesting aspect of his approach is a philosophical rejection of the commercial logic which has so impinged on contemporary architecture. As he says, »A resistance to commercialism and repetition is not only necessary, it is essential to a culture of architecture«.

Steven Holl (* 1947) sagt von sich, daß er auf der Suche nach dem »schwer faßlichen Wesen der Architektur« sei. So bezeichnete auch der japanische Architekt Toyo Ito Holls Bauten als »eher hörbar denn sichtbar«. Diese Idee mag durch Holls eigene Beschreibung des Stretto House (Dallas, Texas, 1989-92) bestätigt werden, worin er Parallelen zwischen diesem Haus und Bartóks »Musik für Streicher, Schlagzeug und Celesta« zieht. In Holls Werk schwingt ein zarter, abstrakter Rhythmus mit, wodurch es sich deutlich von Le Corbusiers Arbeiten absetzt, der zweifellos den größten Einfluß auf Holl ausübte. Ein anderer interessanter Aspekt ist die philosophisch begründete Ablehnung kommerzieller Erwägungen, die die zeitgenössische Architektur stark beeinflußt haben. Mit Holls Worten: » Der Widerstand gegen Kommerz und ständige Wiederholung ist nicht nur notwendig, er ist wesentlich für eine Kultur der Architektur.«

Né en 1947, Steven Holl a déclaré qu'il recherchait: «l'essence élusive de l'architecture». L'architecte japonais Toyo Ito a pu dire des constructions de Holl qu'elles étaient «plus sonores que visuelles». Cette idée est confirmée par la description que donne l'architecte lui-même de sa Stretto House (Dallas, Texas, 1989-92), pour laquelle il trace un parallèle entre la maison et la «Musique pour cordes, percussion et célesta» de Bartók. Il existe un rythme subtil et abstrait dans l'œuvre de Holl qui la différencie en fin de compte de celle de Le Corbusier, sans doute sa principale source d'influence. Un autre aspect intéressant de son approche est le rejet philosophique de la logique commerciale qui exerce une telle pression sur l'architecture contemporaine. Il a ainsi pu dire: «Une résistance au commercial et à la répétition n'est pas seulement nécessaire, elle est essentielle à une culture de l'architecture.»

Stretto House, Dallas, Texas, 1989-92

Ideas, not forms or styles, present the most promising legacy of 20th century architecture.

Vorstellungen, nicht Formen oder Stile sind das vielversprechendste Erbe der Architektur des 20. Jahrhunderts.

Les idées et non les formes et les styles seront le legs le plus prometteur de l'architecture du XXème siècle.

STEVEN HOLL

STRETTO HOUSE 1989-92
DALLAS, TEXAS

Holl says that the structure of this 600 square meter house is based on Béla Bartók's »Music for Strings, Percussion and Celeste«. A »stretto« is an overlapping and building of musical themes, and the spaces of this house do overlap each other. The rhythm of spaces is also established by four small dams which existed on the site. Simple materials such as concrete blocks and white plaster are used with great attention to craftsmanship. Proportions are calculated with reference to golden sections.

Laut Steven Holl basiert die Struktur des 600 m² großen Hauses auf Béla Bartóks »Musik für Streicher, Schlagzeug und Celesta«. »Stretto« bedeutet Überlappen und Herausbilden von musikalischen Themen – entsprechend überlappen sich die Räume. Der Rhythmus der Räume wird auch durch vier kleine, bereits vorhandene Dämme vorgegeben. Handwerklich geschickt wurden einfache Materialien wie Beton und weißer Putz verarbeitet. Die Proportionen entsprechen den Maßstäben des Goldenen Schnitts.

Pour Holl, la structure de cette maison de 600 mètres carrés lui a été inspirée par la «Musique pour cordes, percussions et célesta» de Béla Bartók. Un «stretto» est une accélération et une imbrication de thèmes musicaux et les espaces de cette maison s'imbriquent bien en effet. Leur rythme est également déterminé par quatre petites digues pré-existantes. Des matériaux simples, comme des blocs de béton et du plâtre blanc, sont utilisés avec un grand soin de mise en œuvre. Les proportions sont de la section d'or.

A flowing of spaces related to the adjoining stream connects this house to its site. Sections and elevations demonstrate the interpenetration of spaces and the use of a freely curving roof.

Ineinander übergehende Räume spielen auf den angrenzenden Bach an und verbinden das Haus mit seinem Grundstück. Schnitte und Ansichten zeigen die Durchdringung der Räume und die freie, geschwungene Dachkonstruktion.

L'écoulement des espaces rappelle le torrent contigu et relie la maison au site. Les coupes et les élévations montrent l'interpénétration des espaces et le dessin très libre des courbes du toit.

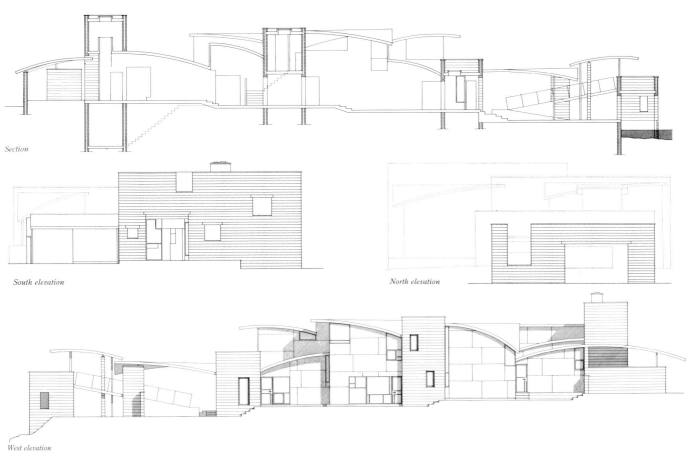

Section

South elevation

North elevation

West elevation

BERLIN AGB LIBRARY (COMPETITION) 1988
BERLIN, GERMANY

Steven Holl compares this addition to the Amerika Gedenkbibliothek to an urban element such as a city gate. A notable feature of the project is a childrens' library with sloping floors »for reading while lying down«, consisting of a lattice truss, sheathed in sandblasted glass, and suspended above an existing building. The interior spaces are conceived for the comfort of the user, as seen in the open stacks with a »browsing circuit«, a path intended to present the entire library.

Steven Holl vergleicht seinen Anbau der Amerika Gedenkbibliothek mit einem städtebaulichen Element wie etwa einem Stadttor. Ein charakteristisches Merkmal dieses Projektes ist eine Bibliothek für Kinder mit schrägen Böden, »um im Liegen lesen zu können«, die aus einem Gittergerüst mit Milchglasscheiben besteht und über einem anderen Gebäude zu hängen scheint. Die wichtigste Planungsgrundlage für den Innenraum bildete der Benutzerkomfort: offene Regale und ein »Spazierweg« durch die Bibliothek.

Steven Holl compare cette extension de l'Amerika Gedenkbibliothek à un élément urbain du type porte de ville. Une des caractéristiques de ce projet est la bibliothèque pour enfants au sol en pente «pour lire en étant couché», construite dans un treillis pris dans une enveloppe de verre sablé et suspendue au dessus d'un bâtiment préexistant. Les espaces intérieurs sont conçus pour le confort de l'utilisateur: des rayonnages ouverts et un «circuit de flânerie», permettant de voir toute la bibliothèque.

The concept of the »browsing circuit« and the open stacks of the library are clearly visible in Holl's drawings, and the model shows how the project absorbs the existing building.

In Holls Zeichnung werden das Konzept des »Spazierwegs« und die offenen Regale deutlich. Das Modell zeigt, wie sich geplanter und bestehender Bau ineinanderfügen.

Le concept du «circuit de flânerie» et les rayonnages ouverts sont clairement visibles sur les dessins de Holl et la maquette montre la façon dont le projet «absorbe» le bâtiment existant.

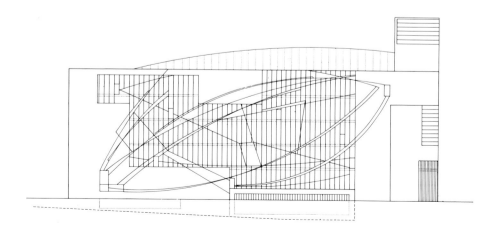

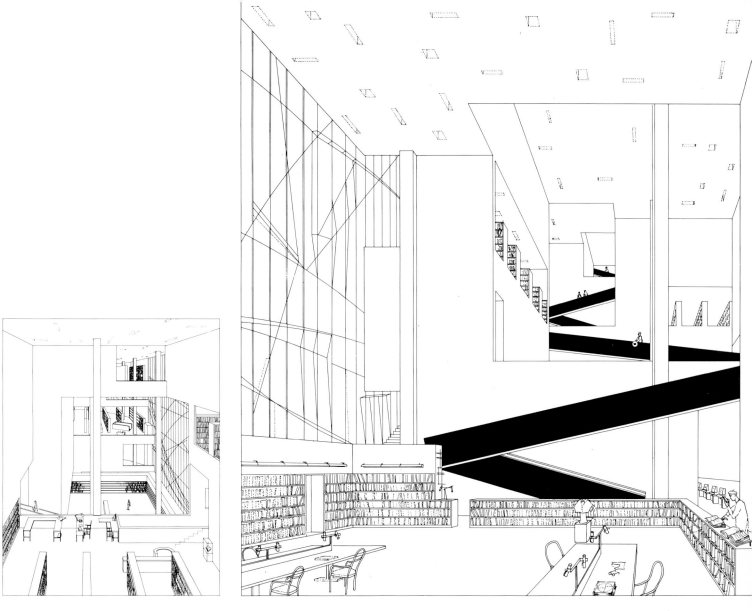

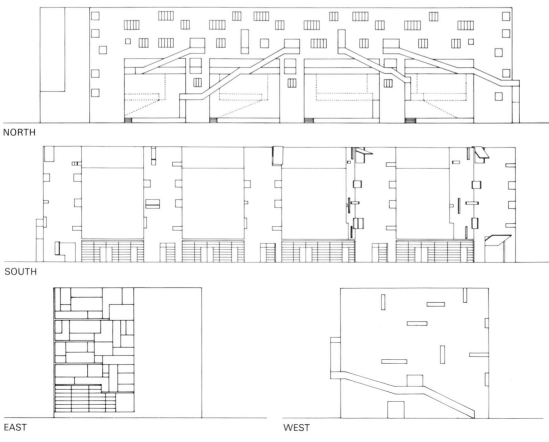

NORTH

SOUTH

EAST

WEST

Elevations and sections reveal the patterns of aluminum and concrete used by the architect in a limited grey and black palette. The emptiness of the interior corresponds to Japanese taste.

Ansichten und Schnitte zeigen die wechselnden Muster aus Aluminium und Beton, die vom Architekten in einer beschränkten Palette von Grau- und Schwarztönen verwendet wurden. Die Leere der Innenräume entspricht japanischem Geschmack.

Les élévations et les coupes montrent le contraste entre l'aluminium et le béton choisis par l'architecte dans une palette réduite au gris et au noir. Le dépouillement de l'intérieur répond au goût japonais.

VOID SPACE/HINGED SPACE, HOUSING 1989-91
NEXUS WORLD, FUKUOKA, JAPAN

This 28 apartment structure is part of the Nexus World project, which has brought several leading western architects to this prosperous city on the island of Kyushu. Concrete and aluminum curtain walls are used to create an almost austere alternation of open and full spaces, relieved only by a slight curve in the floor plans, which is related to the shape of the site. It would seem that the severity of this design is appropriate to the Japanese sense of space, light and emptiness.

Das Gebäude mit 28 Apartments ist Teil des Nexus World Projektes, das verschiedene führende westliche Architekten in diese blühende Stadt auf der Insel Kyushu brachte. Vorgesetzte Fassaden (Curtain Walls) aus Beton und Aluminium erzeugen einen geradezu nüchternen Wechsel aus offenen und geschlossenen Räumen. Dies wurde nur durch eine leichte Rundung in den Grundrissen aufgelockert, die durch die Form des Grundstücks vorgegeben ist. Die Strenge des Entwurfs entspricht dem japanischen Gefühl von Raum, Licht und Leere.

Cet immeuble de 28 appartements fait partie du projet Nexus World qui a permis à plusieurs grands architectes occidentaux d'intervenir sur l'île de Kyushu. Les murs-rideaux de béton et d'aluminium créent une alternance presque austère d'espaces ouverts et fermés, uniquement animés par une courbe figurant sur le plan masse et qui suit la topographie du site. Il semblerait que la sévérité de cette conception corresponde au sens japonais de l'espace, de la lumière et du dépouillement.

HELMUT **JAHN**

Born 1940 in Nuremberg, Germany, Helmut Jahn has brought a dynamic image to large-scale public projects, and specifically to office towers, through the use of up-to-date technology, and a style which recalls 1920's and 1930's Art Deco. Based in the Midwest, he has made the difficult transition from a European background to a successful career in the United States, building major structures in Chicago, New York, Philadelphia and Frankfurt. One of the peculiarities of his design process is the way in which he uses drawings – accumulating various solutions on large sheets of paper. These drawings show the extent to which he implicates himself in each project, and demonstrate why he is not merely a commercial architect, but also an interesting designer who may be having more impact on the skyline of modern cities than anyone else of his generation.

Der 1940 in Nürnberg geborene Helmut Jahn verlieh öffentlichen Großprojekten und vor allem Bürogebäuden ein neues, dynamisches Äußeres. Dabei bediente er sich neuester Bautechniken und eines Stils, der an das Art deco der zwanziger und dreißiger Jahre erinnert. Ausgehend von seinen europäischen Wurzeln hat er den schwierigen Wandel hin zu einer erfolgreichen Karriere in den USA gemeistert und arbeitet heute im mittleren Westen. Er zeichnet verantwortlich für wichtige Bauten in Chicago, New York, Philadelphia und Frankfurt. Eine Besonderheit seines Entwurfsprozesses liegt in den Zeichnungen – die Zusammenstellung verschiedener Lösungen auf großen Entwurfbögen. Diese Zeichnungen zeigen, wie sehr er sich in jedes seiner Projekte einbringt, und demonstrieren, daß er nicht nur ein kommerziell denkender Architekt, sondern ein engagierter Designer ist, der die Skyline moderner Städte vielleicht stärker beeinflußte als jeder andere Architekt seiner Generation.

Né à Nuremberg (Allemagne) en 1940, Helmut Jahn a apporté une dynamique nouvelle à d'importants projets publics et en particulier à des tours de bureaux grâce au recours à une technologie d'avant-garde et à un style qui rappelle le mouvement Art-Déco des annés 20 et 30. Etabli dans le Midwest, il a réussi la transition difficile entre une culture européenne et une carrière américaine réussie, construisant d'importants immeubles à Chicago, New York, Philadelphie et Francfort-sur-le-Main. L'une des particularités de son processus de création est la façon dont il se sert du dessin, accumulant de multiples solutions sur de grandes feuilles de papier. Ces dessins montrent à quel point il s'implique personnellement dans chaque projet et prouvent qu'il n'est pas seulement un architecte commercial mais un créateur intéressant qui aura peut-être plus d'influence sur le paysage urbain de nombreuses villes que beaucoup d'autres architectes de sa génération.

Terminal 1 Complex – United Airlines, O'Hare International Airport, Chicago, Illinois, 1983-87

Every generation must build its own city.

Jede Generation sollte ihre eigene Stadt bauen.

Chaque génération doit construire sa propre cité.

HELMUT JAHN

MESSETURM FRANKFURT 1985-91
FRANKFURT AM MAIN, GERMANY

With its 251 meters, the Messeturm is the tallest office building in Europe. Its total floor area is 85,000 square meters. According to Jahn, the height of the building was dictated by total space requirements and the German regulations that office workers must be near a window, rather than by a desire to build a very tall building. But it remains a symbol. Helmut Jahn affirms here the vocabulary of new Art Deco inspired shapes for skyscrapers, which he had evolved in projects in the U.S.

Mit seinen 251 Metern ist der Messeturm das höchste Bürogebäude Europas. Er hat eine Gesamtfläche von 85 000 m². Laut Jahn wurde die Höhe durch den Raumbedarf und deutsche Vorschriften vorgegeben, die für Büroangestellte einen Arbeitsplatz in Fensternähe vorsehen. Es stand also nicht der Wunsch des Architekten im Vordergrund, ein extrem hohes Gebäude zu entwerfen. Trotzdem behält der Turm Symbolcharakter. Helmut Jahn bekräftigt hier die Sprache der durch ein neues Art deco inspirierten Wolkenkratzer, die er in den USA entwickelt hat.

Avec ses 251 m, la «Messeturm» est l'immeuble le plus haut d'Europe. Sa surface développée totale est de 85 000 mètres carrés. Selon Jahn, cette hauteur lui a été dictée par le besoin de surface du client et la réglementation allemande, qui veut que les employés se trouvent près d'une fenêtre, plutôt que par le désir de construire une tour de grande hauteur. Celle-ci est néanmoins devenue un symbole. Helmut Jahn affirme ici le vocabulaire d'essence Art-Déco qu'il a développé dans plusieurs projets aux USA.

This drawing (below) of an early design shows the exhibition hall, the tower, and the 1909 Festhalle, by F. von Thiersch. To the right, a typical sketch sheet shows Jahn's design process.

Diese frühe Zeichnung (unten) zeigt die Ausstellungshalle, den Turm und die Festhalle von 1909 von F. von Thiersch. Rechts: Das typische Zeichenblatt zeigt Jahns Entwurfsprozeß.

Dessin (en bas) d'un premier projet montrant la salle d'exposition, la tour et la salle des fêtes de F. von Thiersch (1909). A droite, un exemple typique du processus de dessin de Jahn.

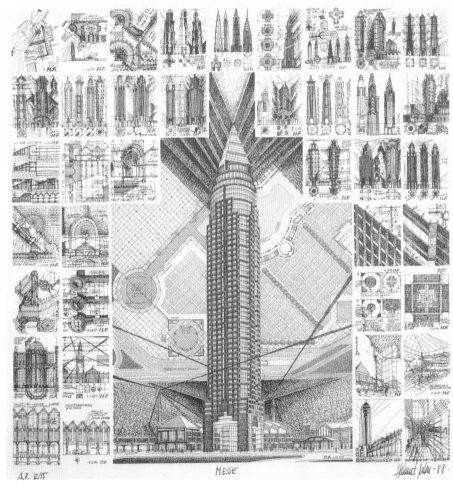

TERMINAL 1 COMPLEX – UNITED AIRLINES 1983-87
O'HARE INTERNATIONAL AIRPORT, CHICAGO, ILLINOIS

More than 100,000 square meters of operating facilities, 48 gates and two main structures, each about 490 meters long, linked by a 250 meter underground passageway. The statistics speak for themselves in this project, which is part of the O'Hare Development Program. Typically, Helmut Jahn has blended a meticulous attention to technical details, an analysis of passenger flow and his dramatic sense of space and movement. He proves again that modern architecture can have great flexibility.

Mehr als 100 000 m² Betriebseinrichtungen, 48 Flugsteige und zwei Hauptgebäude, jedes davon 490 Meter lang, verbunden durch einen 250 Meter langen unterirdischen Korridor. Die statistischen Zahlen dieses Projekts, das Teil des Entwicklungsprogramms für den O'Hare-Flughafen ist, sprechen für sich. Helmut Jahn hat in typischer Weise genaueste Beachtung technischer Details mit einer Analyse der Passagierströme und seinem Gefühl für Raum und Bewegung verbunden. Er beweist einmal mehr, daß moderne Architektur sehr flexibel sein kann.

Plus de 100 000 mètres carrés d'installations, 48 portes et deux bâtiments principaux, chacun de 490 m de long, reliés par un passage souterrain de 250 m: les chiffres parlent d'eux-mêmes pour ce projet qui fait partie du programme d'extension de O'Hare. Typiquement, Helmut Jahn a marié une attention méticuleuse aux détails techniques et une analyse approfondie des flux de passagers à son sens spectaculaire de l'espace et du mouvement. Il prouve une fois de plus que l'architecture moderne peut faire preuve d'une grande souplesse.

The long concourses of the Terminal are designed to give visual variety and a sense of movement. A plan to the right shows the juxtaposition of the two main buildings, which are linked underground.

Der Entwurf der langen Gänge des Flughafens vermittelt optische Vielfalt und den Eindruck von Bewegung. Der Plan rechts zeigt die Lage der zwei Hauptgebäude zueinander, die unterirdisch miteinander verbunden sind.

Les longs bâtiments du Terminal sont conçus pour éviter la monotonie visuelle et donner un sens du mouvement. Le plan de droite montre la juxtaposition des deux principaux bâtiments reliés par un souterrain.

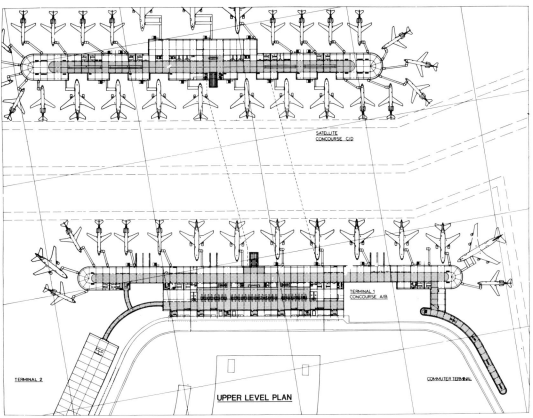

SATELLITE
CONCOURSE C/D

TERMINAL 1
CONCOURSE A/B

TERMINAL 2

COMMUTER TERMINAL

UPPER LEVEL PLAN

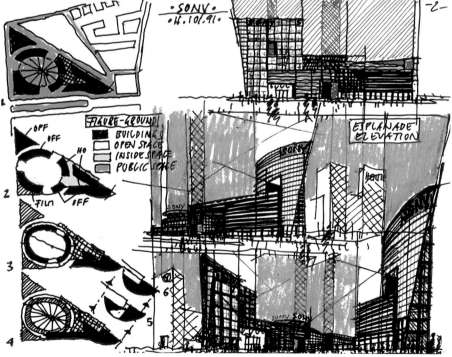

Helmut Jahn's work is recognizable through his dramatic use of modern forms and high technology. Together with park space, and public passages, the Sony-Forum (right page) will certainly attract crowds.

Helmut Jahns Arbeiten zeichnen sich durch innovative Formensprache und modernste Technik aus. Zusammen mit dem Parkhaus und den Passagen wird das Sony-Forum (rechte Seite) sicherlich Scharen von Besuchern anlocken.

L'œuvre d'Helmut Jahn se caractérise par le recours à des formes modernes spectaculaires et une technologie avancée. Avec son parc et ses passages publiques, le Sony-Forum (page de droite) devrait attirer des foules nombreuses.

SONY CENTER 1995
BERLIN, GERMANY

Along with Sony's European Headquarters, this 200,000 square meter complex will house offices, a cinema, a cultural complex, a hotel, shops and apartments. Designed to respond to its urban environment, near the Potsdamer Platz, the building will be clad in stone, metal and glass in a grey-black to silver color scheme. For the public, the defining space will be the Sony-Forum, a vast »covered-open« area, under a cable, membrane and glass »umbrella«, where there will be live or video entertainment.

Zusammen mit der Hauptverwaltung von Sony Europa wird dieser 200 000 m² große Komplex Büroräume, ein Kino, ein Kulturzentrum, ein Hotel, Läden und Apartments enthalten. Das Gebäude soll mit Stein, Metallplatten und Glas in grau-schwarzen und silbrigen Farbtönen verkleidet werden und ist so entworfen, daß es mit der urbanen Umgebung am Potsdamer Platz korrespondiert. Der für die Öffentlichkeit bestimmte Bereich, das sogenannte Sony-Forum, ist als »halboffene« Zone geplant, in der unter einem »Schirm« aus Seilen, Segeltuch und Glas Live- oder Video-Unterhaltung geboten werden soll.

Parallèlement au siège européen de Sony, ce complexe de 200 000 mètres carrés accueillera des bureaux, un cinéma, un centre culturel, un hôtel, des magasins et des appartements. Conçu pour s'intégrer dans l'environnement urbain de la Potsdamer Platz, le bâtiment sera recouvert de pierre, de métal et de verre dans des tons allant de gris-noir à argent. Pour le public, l'espace marquant sera le Sony-Forum, une vaste zone «couverte/ouverte», abritée par un parapluie de verre, de résine synthétique et de câbles sous lequel se donneront des spectacles vidéo ou en direct.

RICHARD **MEIER**

A member of the »New York Five«, Richard Meier (* 1934) has been an architect whose consistent, some would even say obsessional use of Modernist white forms has become a universally recognizable signature style. Influenced by Le Corbusier, Meier has proven that a gridded, geometrical vocabulary is capable of an astonishing variety of types of expression. Initially on a small scale, for numerous private residences, and later in progressively larger commissions, office buildings, museums or housing, he has evolved toward more complex floor plans, and a shifting of axes which has come to be considered typical of much contemporary architecture. It remains to be seen if the largest project of his career, the Getty Center in Los Angeles, scheduled for completion in 1996, will confirm his reputation as one of the most outstanding architects of his generation.

Die konsequente, von einigen auch als »besessen« bezeichnete Verwendung weißer Baukörper gilt als das Markenzeichen Richard Meiers (* 1934), einem Mitglied der »New York Five«. Der von Le Corbusier beeinflußte Architekt hat bewiesen, daß auch gitterartige geometrische Baukörper vielfältige Ausdrucksmöglichkeiten bieten. Meier begann in kleinem Rahmen mit zahlreichen Privathäusern und entwickelte später bei größeren Aufträgen für Verwaltungsgebäude, Museen oder Wohnanlagen immer kompliziertere Grundrisse und Achsenverschiebungen, die heute als typisch für einen Teil zeitgenössischer Architektur angesehen werden können. Es bleibt abzuwarten, ob das bisher größte Projekt seiner Karriere, das neue Getty Center in Los Angeles, dessen Fertigstellung für 1996 geplant ist, seinen Ruf als einen der wichtigsten Architekten unserer Zeit bestätigen wird.

Membre des «New York Five», Richard Meier (né en 1934) est l'un des architectes dont le recours permanent, certains diront obsessionnel, à des formes blanches d'esprit moderniste est devenu une signature identifiable dans le monde entier. Influencé par Le Corbusier, Meier a prouvé qu'un vocabulaire géométrique fondé sur une grille était capable d'une variété étonnante d'expressions. Travaillant initialement sur de petits projets, pour de nombreuses résidences privées, et plus tard pour des commandes de plus en plus importantes, il a évolué vers une plus grande complexité de plans et vers un glissement d'axes devenu typique pour un partie des œuvres de l'architecture contemporaine. Il reste à vérifier si le plus grand projet de sa carrière, le nouveau Getty Center de Los Angeles, qui devrait ouvrir en 1996, confirmera sa réputation d'être l'un des plus brillants architectes de sa génération.

Canal Plus Headquarters, Paris, France, 1989-92

White is the ephemeral emblem of perpetual movement.

Weiß ist das flüchtige Symbol ewiger Bewegung.

Le blanc est l'emblème éphémère du mouvement perpétuel.

RICHARD MEIER

MUSEUM FOR THE DECORATIVE ARTS 1979-85
FRANKFURT AM MAIN, GERMANY

Located on the Main opposite the downtown area, along the »Museumsufer«, this Museum integrates the typically 19th century Villa Metzler into its design. The purity of some façades and internal details like ship-railing, recall Meier's attachment, as part of the New York Five, to the work of Le Corbusier. But here, a rotated grid, and complex forms declare the contemporary nature of the architecture. The rigorous concept may not, however, be ideally suited to the display of decorative arts.

Am Museumsufer, direkt am Main gegenüber der Innenstadt gelegen, bezieht das Museum für Kunsthandwerk die für das 19. Jahrhundert typische Villa Metzler mit in seinen Entwurf ein. Die Strenge der Fassaden und kleine Details im Inneren wie die relingartigen Handläufe erinnern an Meiers Zugehörigkeit zu den New York Five und an seine Verbindung zu Le Corbusier. Hier weisen jedoch die umlaufende Gitterstruktur und die komplexeren Formen auf den zeitgenössischen Charakter seiner Arbeit hin. Dabei paßt das strenge Konzept nicht immer zur Präsentation von Kunsthandwerk.

Situé au bord du Main face au centre ancien et sur la Museumsufer, ce musée intègre la Villa Metzler, typique d'un certain style XIXème allemand. La pureté des façades et des détails intérieurs, comme les rambardes de navire, rappellent l'attachement de Meier, et des «New York Five», à l'œuvre de Le Corbusier. Ici, une trame basculée et des formes complexes affirment l'esprit contemporain de cette architecture. Ce concept rigoureux s'adapte parfois avec difficulté à la présentation des arts décoratifs.

Combining rigorous lines with his usual white cladding, Meier creates a jewel-like perfection.

Durch die Verbindung von strenger Linienführung und weißem Putz schuf Meier ein Gebäude von einzigartiger Perfektion.

En combinant des lignes rigoureuses à son célèbre revêtement blanc, Meier atteint ici à une précision d'orfèvre.

CANAL PLUS HEADQUARTERS
1989-92
PARIS, FRANCE

Designed for a pay television group, this building is one of the most successful modern additions to Paris in recent years. Located on the banks of the Seine, near the new André Citroën park, the building maintains a delicately articulated appearance, despite its more than 35,000 square meters in floor area. Clad in Meier's trademark white, the building stands out like a high-tech beacon which reminds visitors that the influence of Le Corbusier continues to mark architecture.

Das Gebäude wurde für einen kommerziellen Fernsehsender entworfen und zählt zu den aufsehenerregendsten Neubauten der letzten Jahre in Paris. Obwohl das am Ufer der Seine in der Nähe des André Citroën Park gelegene Gebäude eine Grundfläche von über 35000 m² einnimmt, erweckt es dennoch den Eindruck von Leichtigkeit. Es erstrahlt wie ein Signal des High-Tech in Meiers typischem Weiß und erinnert den Besucher an den Einfluß, den Le Corbusier bis heute auf die Architektur ausübt.

Conçu pour une chaîne de télévision payante, ce bâtiment est l'une des œuvres architecturales les plus réussies dont Paris ait bénéficié ces dernières années. Implantée sur la rive gauche de la Seine, près du nouveau Parc André Citroën, la construction s'articule avec délicatesse malgré sa complexité et ses 35000 mètres carrés. Recouverte d'un matériau blanc pur, marque distinctive de Meier, elle se dresse comme une balise high-tech qui signalerait aux passants que l'influence de Le Corbusier marque encore l'architecture de notre époque.

A narrow office wing, with a large opening runs along the Seine, while production facilities, studios and a theater are located on a perpendicular axis.

Ein schlanker Verwaltungsflügel mit einer großen Öffnung erstreckt sich entlang der Seine. Die Produktionseinrichtungen, die Studios und ein Theater sind auf einer senkrechten Achse dazu untergebracht.

Une aile étroite réservée aux bureaux et se terminant par une grande ouverture court le long de la Seine, tandis que les installations de production, les studios et la salle de spectacles sont implantés selon un axe perpendiculaire.

THE GETTY CENTER 1984-96
LOS ANGELES, CALIFORNIA

This 50 hectare complex for the wealthiest art trust is one of the most ambitious projects of the decade. Located on a hilltop along the San Diego Freeway, the complex will include a central administrative building, a Center for the History of Art and the Humanities, a 450 seat auditorium, a large museum, food services and numerous satellite facilities. The whole, likened to the Villa Hadriana or to the Acropolis, is to be clad not in Meier's favorite white, but in cleft travertine.

Der 50 Hektar große Komplex der wohlhabenden Kunststiftung gilt als eines der ehrgeizigsten Projekte dieser Dekade. Auf einem Berg am San Diego Freeway entstehen ein zentrales Verwaltungsgebäude, ein Zentrum für Kunstgeschichte und Gesellschaftwissenschaften, ein Hörsaal mit 450 Plätzen, ein großes Museum, Restaurants und verschiedene Satelliteneinrichtungen. Das Projekt soll nicht mit den von Meier bevorzugten weißen Platten verkleidet werden, sondern mit Travertin, ähnlich wie die Villa Hadriana und die Akropolis.

Cet ensemble de 50 ha édifié pour la fondation artistique la plus riche du monde est un des projets les plus ambitieux de la décennie. Situé au sommet d'une colline le long de l'autoroute de San Diego, l'ensemble comprendra un bâtiment administratif central, un centre pour l'histoire de l'Art et les Humanités, un auditorium de 450 places, un grand musée, des restaurants et de nombreuses installations complémentaires. Déjà comparé à la Villa d'Hadrien ou à l'Acropole, il sera recouvert de travertin et non des panneaux blancs qu'affectionne Meier.

Designed in harmony with the topography of the site, the Getty Center is limited in height because of the activism of local residents.

Das Getty Center harmoniert mit der Umgebung und ist aufgrund einer Anwohner-Initiative in der Bauhöhe begrenzt.

Intégré à la topographie du site, le Getty Center est limité en hauteur par l'activisme des voisins.

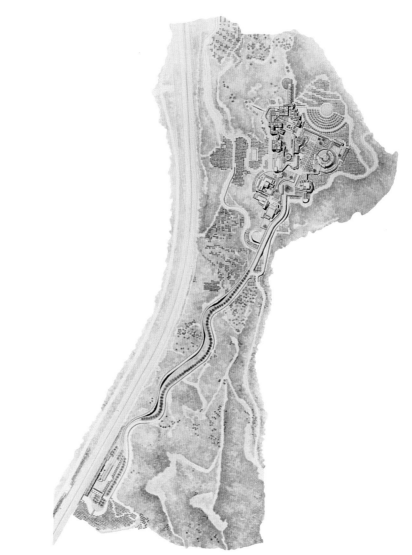

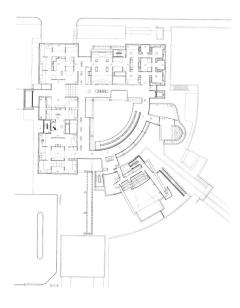

HIGH MUSEUM OF ART 1980-83
ATLANTA, GEORGIA

Situated three kilometers from downtown Atlanta, this is one of Richard Meier's first and strongest museum projects. The powerful bulk of the structure is alleviated by large glass façades and an entrance ramp, which reaches out to the visitor. Meier admits that the central atrium of the building was inspired by Frank Lloyd Wright's Guggenheim Museum. White porcelain-enameled steel panels clad many exterior façades, and the 13,000 square meter building includes about 5000 square meters of gallery space.

Dieses drei Kilometer außerhalb der Innenstadt von Atlanta gelegene Gebäude gilt als eines von Meiers ersten und auch besten Museumsprojekten. Die geballte Masse des Baukörpers wird durch große Glasfassaden und eine Rampe aufgelockert, die eine Verbindung zum Besucher schafft. Das zentrale Atrium des Gebäudes ist laut Meier von Frank Lloyd Wrights Guggenheim Museum beeinflußt. Weiße emaillierte Stahlplatten verkleiden einen Großteil der äußeren Fassade; die Gesamtfläche von 13 000 m² umfaßt etwa 5000 m² Ausstellungsfläche.

A trois kilomètres du centre ville, ce musée est l'un des premiers et plus brillants projets muséaux de Richard Meier. Le puissant volume de la structure est allégé par de vastes façades de verre et une rampe d'entrée, qui va littéralement chercher le visiteur. Meier admet que l'atrium central lui a été inspiré par le Guggenheim Museum de Frank Lloyd Wright. Des panneaux émaillés de porcelaine blanche recouvrent les façades extérieures et les 13 000 mètres carrés du bâtiment comprennent environ 5000 mètres carrés d'espaces d'exposition.

The main entrance ramp leads to the heart of the structure, which is the large glassed-in atrium visible in the photo below. The galleries are designed to give multiple points of view on the art.

Die Rampe des Haupteinganges führt in das Zentrum des Bauwerks: ein großes gläsernes Atrium (unten). Die Galerien sind so entworfen, daß sie viele verschiedene Blickwinkel auf die Kunstwerke freigeben.

La rampe de l'entrée principale mène au cœur de la structure qui est le vaste atrium de verre visible sur la photo ci-dessus. Les galeries sont conçues pour offrir de multiples points de vue sur les œuvres.

CHARLES **MOORE**

Charles Moore (* 1925) has said that architecture should be considered a performing art. Indeed, some of his projects, like the famous Piazza d'Italia (New Orleans, Louisiana, 1977-78) or the Wonderwall (World's Fair, New Orleans, Louisiana, 1982-84) look more like stage designs than they bring to mind »serious« architecture. Because of his frequent changes of style, Charles Moore escapes any easy classification. But it is apparent that through his extensive body of built work and his teaching across the United States (University of California, Yale, University of Texas) he has had a considerable influence on American architecture in the past thirty years. It was certainly the IBA competition for the Tegel Harbor Housing (1980) which brought Charles Moore to international attention. He has also built in Japan (Nishiokamoto Housing, Kobe, Japan, 1992).

Der 1925 geborene Charles Moore sagt, daß Architektur als eine Art Theater betrachtet werden soll. Und so wirken auch einige seiner Projekte wie die bekannte Piazza d'Italia (New Orleans, Louisiana, 1977-78) oder der Wonderwall (Weltausstellung, New Orleans, Louisiana, 1982-84) eher wie Bühnenentwürfe denn als »ernsthafte« Architektur. Durch ständigen Stilwechsel verhindert Charles Moore jegliche Festlegung. Aber es ist offensichtlich, daß er durch die große Menge seiner Bauten und die Lehrtätigkeit an zahlreichen Universitäten (University of California, Yale, University of Texas) einen großen Einfluß auf die amerikanische Architektur der letzten dreißig Jahre hatte. Sein Wettbewerbsbeitrag für die IBA, die Wohnanlage am Tegeler Hafen (1980), brachte Charles Moore internationale Aufmerksamkeit. Ebenso baute er in Kobe, Japan (Nishiokamoto Wohnanlage 1992).

Né en 1925, Charles Moore a un jour déclaré que l'architecture devrait être considérée comme un art de la représentation. En fait, certains de ses projets, comme la fameuse Piazza d'Italia (New Orleans, Louisiane, 1977-78) ou le Wonderwall (World's Fair, New Orleans, Louisiane, 1982-84) font plus penser à des décors de théâtre qu'à une création architecturale «sérieuse». Changeant fréquemment de style, Charles Moore échappe à toute classification. Mais il est certain qu'à travers ses nombreuses constructions et son enseignement à travers tous les Etats-Unis (University of California, Yale, University of Texas) il a exercé une influence considérable sur l'architecture américaine de ces trente dernières années. Le concours de l'IBA pour un projet d'habitations dans le Port de Tegel, à Berlin, a attiré sur lui l'attention internationale. Il a également construit au Japon (Immeuble d'habitation Nishiokamoto, Kobe, Japon, 1992).

Tegel Harbor, Humboldt Bibliothek, Berlin, Germany, 1987-88

We are deeply rooted in culture, places and people. Architecture is part of a continuum.

Wir sind tief verwurzelt in unserer Kultur, in Orten und in Menschen. Architektur ist Teil eines Kontinuums.

Nous sommes enracinés dans une culture, dans un peuple, dans des lieux. L'architecture fait partie d'un continuum.

CHARLES MOORE

The Humboldt Bibliothek (left page) is part of the Tegel Harbor complex (above) with 170 units designed by Moore, and 150 by other architects.

Die Humboldt-Bibliothek (linke Seite) ist Teil des Komplexes am Tegeler Hafen (oben), bei dem 170 Wohneinheiten von Moore und 150 Einheiten von anderen Architekten entworfen wurden.

La Bibliothèque Humboldt (page de gauche) fait partie du complexe du port de Tegel qui compte 170 appartements réalisés par Moore et 150 par d'autres architectes.

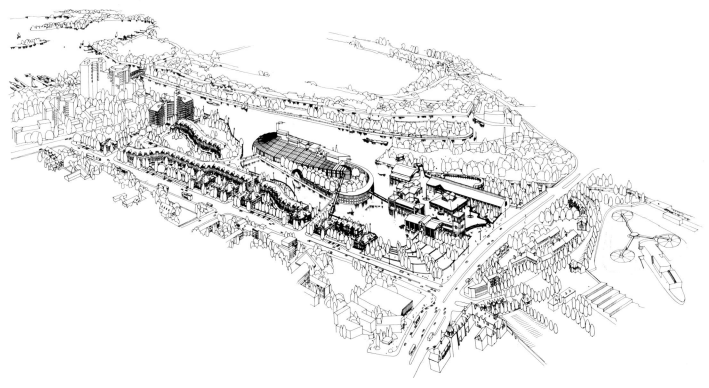

TEGEL HARBOR, PHASE I HOUSING, TEGEL VILLA, HUMBOLDT BIBLIOTHEK 1987-88
BERLIN, GERMANY

Moore calls the style of the Humboldt Bibliothek, the first phase of Tegel Harbor's Cultural Center, »industrial-Baroque«. Steel, concrete and corrugated aluminum are used inside to give an accessible atmosphere to the open stacks. The Tegel Harbor Housing, with 170 units, is part of a complex with a master-plan by Moore Ruble Yudell. A large vocabulary of architectural forms gives this social housing a richly varied aspect, united by the color scheme and the zinc roofing.

Moore bezeichnet den Stil der Humboldt-Bibliothek – der ersten Bauphase des Kulturzentrums am Tegeler Hafen – als »Industrie-Barock«. Stahl, Beton und Wellblech wurden im Inneren verwendet, um eine benutzerfreundliche Atmosphäre zu schaffen. Die Anlage mit 170 Wohneinheiten ist Teil eines größeren Komplexes unter der Leitung von Moore Ruble Yudell. Farbschema und Zinkdächer sind verbunden mit vielfältigen architektonischen Formen.

Moore qualifie le style de la Bibliothèque Humboldt, première phase du centre culturel du port de Tegel, de «baroque industriel». Acier, béton et tôle d'aluminium sont utilisés pour donner à l'intérieur une atmosphère ouverte. Les 170 appartements de l'immeuble d'habitation font partie d'un complexe plus vaste dont le plan masse est dû à Moore Ruble Yudell. Le recours aux formes architecturales très varié donne un aspect très vivant, par le jeu des couleurs et les toits en zinc.

A bell tower (left) indicates that this compound has a religious function. Although walled, the white-washed complex is intended to give a feeling of community and openness.

Die religiöse Bedeutung der Anlage wird durch den Glockenturm (links) unterstrichen. Das Weiß des ummauerten Komplexes soll ein Gefühl von Gemeinschaft und Offenheit vermitteln.

Un clocher (à gauche) signale la fonction religieuse de l'ensemble. Bien qu'entouré de mur ce complexe blanchi à la chaux donne un sentiment de communauté et d'ouverture.

CHURCH OF THE NATIVITY 1989
RANCHO SANTA FE, CALIFORNIA

This church is located in a rural valley north of La Jolla, California. Enclosed in a walled compound, it brings to mind the Spanish religious architecture of the early missionaries. Designed to accommodate future expansions, the church provides for the seating of 550 persons in a fan-shaped pattern. The interior design is relatively simple, with a dominance of white, wooden and terracotta tones. Large openings provide indirect lighting, and there are no stained glass windows.

Die Kirche liegt in einem ländlichen Tal nördlich von La Jolla in Kalifornien. Sie ist eingefügt in einen ummauerten Bezirk und läßt die Erinnerung an religiöse Architektur der frühen spanischen Missionare aufkommen. Mit dem Gedanken an zukünftige Erweiterungen entworfen, bietet die fächerförmige Kirche 550 Personen Platz. Die Inneneinrichtung ist schlicht, wobei Weiß, Holz und Terracotta dominieren. Große Öffnungen sorgen für eine indirekte Beleuchtung ohne Buntglasfenster.

Cette église est située dans une vallée rurale au nord de La Jolla, en Californie. Inscrite dans un ensemble entouré de murs, elle fait penser à l'architecture religieuse des premières missions espagnoles. Prévue pour de futurs agrandissements, l'église peut accueillir 550 personnes assises selon un plan en éventail. L'intérieur est relativement simple, avec une dominante de tons de blanc, de bois et de terre cuite. En l'absence de vitraux, de grandes ouvertures apportent un éclairage indirect.

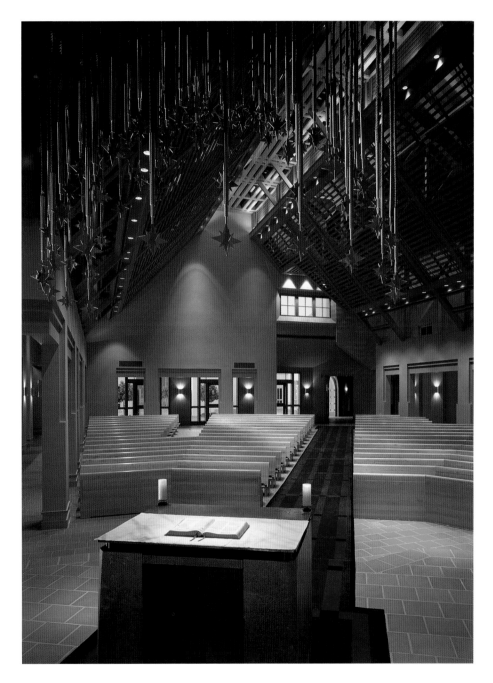

UNIVERSITY OF OREGON SCIENCE COMPLEX 1990
EUGENE, OREGON

The design for this five-building complex was intended to restore architectural unity to a 1914 campus. Housing a library and the departments of geology, physics, biology and computer science, the buildings provide ample common areas such as the four-story atrium, and courtyards. A »science walk« offers an external link between the buildings. The disposition of the various elements took the users' desires into account, as well as the natural relationships which exist between these sciences.

Der Entwurf des fünf Gebäude umfassenden Komplexes sollte die architektonische Einheit der Campusanlage von 1914 wiederherstellen. Die Gebäude beherbergen eine Bibliothek sowie die Fakultäten für Geologie, Physik, Biologie und Informatik. Außerdem bieten sie geräumige öffentliche Bereiche wie das viergeschossige Atrium und verschiedene Innenhöfe. Im Außenbereich sind die Gebäude durch einen »Wissenschaftsweg« verbunden. Bei der Planung wurde Rücksicht auf die Bedürfnisse der Benutzer und auf die Beziehungen der Wissenschaften untereinander genommen.

Le dessin de ce complexe de cinq bâtiments était censé restaurer l'unité architecturale d'un campus datant de 1914. Accueillant une bibliothèque, ainsi que les départements de géologie, de physique, de biologie et d'informatique, les bâtiments offrent de vastes espaces communs comme l'atrium, haut de quatre étages, et différentes cours. Une «promenade des sciences» assure une liaison extérieure entre les constructions. La disposition des divers éléments tient compte des désirs des utilisateurs, de même que des relations naturelles entre les diverses disciplines concernées.

The atrium and courtyards of the brick buildings provide a conviviality and open circulation between the classrooms, conference spaces, research laboratories and institutes.

Das Atrium und die Innenhöfe der Ziegelsteinbauten ermöglichen ein kommunikatives Miteinander und einen Austausch zwischen den Hörsälen, den Konferenzräumen, den Forschungslabors und den Instituten.

L'atrium et les cours des bâtiments en brique permettent une convivialité et une circulation ouverte entre les salles de classe, de conférence, les laboratoires de recherche et les instituts.

MORPHOSIS

The »Modernist penchant for unification and simplification must be broken«, writes Morphosis' principal, Thom Mayne. The work of his group has emphasized the importance of societal changes, such as the growing role of electronic communications, and the »breakdown of a conventional notion of community«. Although based on a different analysis, Morphosis – like certain Japanese architects – has insisted on breaking down the separation of boundaries between the interior and the exterior of buildings. Like Peter Eisenman, they look to chaos theory and other recent scientific thought to explain and to justify the diversity and the apparently disordered forms which they have generated. They have attempted to change the relationship between construction and nature, to make architecture more »supportive« than »dominant«, as in their 1991 Chiba, Japan Golf Club project.

»Die moderne Vorliebe für Vereinheitlichung und Vereinfachung muß zerstört werden«, schreibt der Leiter von Morphosis, Thom Mayne. Die Arbeiten dieser Gruppe betonen die Dominanz sozialer Veränderungen wie die wachsende Bedeutung elektronischer Kommunikation und den »Zusammenbruch der gewohnten Vorstellung vom Zusammenleben«. Obwohl sie von unterschiedlichen Standpunkten ausgehen, beharren die Mitglieder von Morphosis genau wie verschiedene japanische Architekten darauf, die Grenzen des Innen und Außen von Gebäuden aufzuheben. Wie Peter Eisenman ziehen auch sie die Chaos-Theorie und andere wissenschaftliche Theorien dazu heran, ihre scheinbar ungeordneten Entwürfe zu erklären und zu rechtfertigen. Sie versuchen die Beziehung zwischen Konstruktion und Natur zu verändern, um Architektur eher »unterstützend« als »dominant« erscheinen zu lassen – wie etwa in ihrem Chiba, Japan Golf Club Projekt von 1991.

«Le penchant moderniste pour l'unification et la simplification doit être aboli», écrit le responsable de Morphosis, Thom Mayne. L'œuvre de ce groupe met l'accent sur l'importance des changements de la société, tels le rôle grandissant de la communication électronique et «l'effondrement de la conception conventionnelle de la vie en commun». Bien que partant d'une analyse différente, Morphosis insiste, comme certains architectes japonais, sur la supression de la séparation entre l'intérieur et l'extérieur des bâtiments. De même que Peter Eisenman, le groupe s'intéresse à la théorie du chaos et à d'autres pensées scientifiques récentes pour expliquer et justifier la diversité et le désordre apparent de ses formes. Il tente de modifier les relations entre le construit et la nature, pour donner à l'architecture une valeur qui soit plus celle d'un «soutien» que d'une «domination», comme dans son projet pour un club de golf au Japon, Chiba (1991).

Kate Mantilini Restaurant, Beverly Hills, California, 1986

Our work transcribes the fragmented, dispersed, and detached nature of existence.

Unsere Arbeit umschreibt die fragmentarische, zerstreute und zersplitterte Natur des Seins.

Notre travail est une transcription de la nature fragmentée, dispersée et hachée de l'existence.

THOM MAYNE

CEDAR'S SINAI COMPREHENSIVE CANCER CENTER 1987
LOS ANGELES, CALIFORNIA

This is an out-patient facility, added to a large hospital complex. It is built on a difficult site, on and under a parking lot and helipad, with more than half of the space below ground level. A dense, complex building, the center is organized around an atrium and waiting area. It is punctuated by a »play structure« which is characteristic of the exploration of spatial relations implicit in most of the work of Morphosis. Long corridors are intended to permit easy orientation.

Das Krebs-Zentrum ist eine ambulante Einrichtung für Patienten und gehört zu einem großen Krankenhaus-Komplex. Es wurde auf einem schwierigen Gelände gebaut, das zwischen einem Parkhaus und einem Hubschrauberlandeplatz liegt; mehr als die Hälfte der Räume befinden sich unter der Erdoberfläche. Das Center entstand als dichtes, komplexes Gebäude rund um ein Atrium und einen Wartebereich. Sein »spielerischer Aufbau« ist charakteristisch für die Erforschung von räumlichen Beziehungen, die man in den meisten Arbeiten von Morphosis findet. Lange Korridore sollen eine einfache Orientierung ermöglichen.

Ce Centre est un service pour patients extérieurs qui complète un vaste ensemble hospitalier. Il est construit sur un site difficile – au-dessus et en dessous d'un parking et d'un héliport – et plus de la moitié de sa surface se trouve en sous-sol. Bâtiment dense et complexe, il s'organise autour d'un atrium et d'une zone d'attente. Il est ponctué par une «structure ludique» caractéristique de cette exploration des relations spatiales implicite dans la plupart des travaux de Morphosis. De longs corridors sont censés permettre une orientation plus facile.

Located in large part below grade, the Center seems to rise up out of the ground, and the waiting area, with its »play structure« does indeed extend from a lower level up towards the daylight.

Das Krebs-Zentrum scheint aus dem Boden herauszuwachen, da es zum großen Teil unter der Oberfläche liegt; der Wartebereich mit seinem »spielerischen Aufbau« dehnt sich von einer tieferen Ebene hin zum Tageslicht aus.

En grande partie souterrain, le Centre semble s'élever du sol et la zone d'attente et sa «structure ludique» se déploient en effet du niveau inférieur vers la lumière.

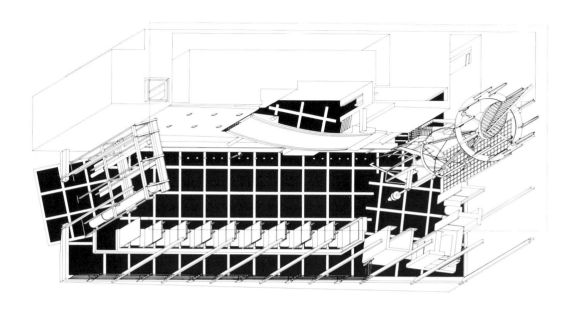

KATE MANTILINI RESTAURANT

1986

BEVERLY HILLS, CALIFORNIA

Located on a busy corner of Wilshire Boulevard, this project is a conversion of a 600 square meter bank office, into a restaurant. Rather than erasing all trace of the earlier structure, Morphosis engulfed elements of its façade. The interior of this »roadside steakhouse for the future« is an open space lit by lateral windows and an overhead oculus. Although not overtly incongruous, the design indulges in unexpected shifts.

Für das Projekt, das an einer belebten Ecke des Wilshire Boulevard liegt, wurde eine 600 m² große ehemalige Bank in ein Restaurant verwandelt. Anstatt alle Spuren des früheren Gebäudes zu beseitigen, integrierte Morphosis Elemente der ehemaligen Fassade in den aktuellen Entwurf. Das Innere des »Steakhauses der Zukunft am Straßenrand« bildet ein offener Raum, in den das Licht durch seitliche Fenster und ein Ochsenauge in der Decke einfällt. Auch wenn der Entwurf keine Widersprüche zeigt, arbeitet er doch mit überraschenden Wandlungen.

Ce projet consistait à transformer les 600 mètres carrés d'une agence bancaire située à un carrefour animé de Wilshire Boulevard en restaurant. Plutôt que d'effacer toute trace de la structure pré-existante, Morphosis a conservé en les englobant des éléments de sa façade. L'intérieur de ce «Grill routier pour le futur» est un espace ouvert, éclairé par des fenêtres latérales et un oculus zénithal. Bien qu'il ne soit pas incohérent, le dessin se permet des décalages inattendus.

Though details evoke the strict modernism of neighboring structures, the Mantilini Restaurant offers numerous surprises, including the 4 meter interior oculus, and »conceptual structure« beneath it.

Das Mantilini Restaurant bietet im Gegensatz zur strengen Moderne der benachbarten Gebäude viele Überraschungen. Dazu gehören das Ochsenauge im Inneren des Gebäudes mit einem Durchmesser von vier Metern ebenso wie das »Konzeptbauwerk« darunter.

Si de nombreux détails rappellent le strict minimalisme des constructions voisines, le Restaurant Mantilini offre de nombreuses surprises, dont un oculus intérieur de 4 mètres de haut et une «structure conceptuelle» placée juste en dessous.

ERIC OWEN **MOSS**

The architect Philip Johnson calls Eric Owen Moss (* 1943) »a jeweler of junk.« In his work built to date, this young California architect has placed an emphasis on unusual materials. Old chains, broken trusses and other incongruous elements take their place in his buildings, much as they might participate in a modern sculpture. The visual arts have acquired a freedom which seemed forbidden to architecture because of the constraints of practicality and building codes, but also because of peoples' »expectations«. Like the Austrian Wolf Prix, principal of the Coop Himmelblau firm, who praises his work, Eric Owen Moss is in the process of exploring the ways in which architecture can be »de-constructed«. His own peculiarity, as evidenced in the buildings he has completed in Culver City, California, remains his extensive, and unexpected experimentation with materials and forms.

Der Architekt Philip Johnson nannte Eric Owen Moss (* 1943) den »Juwelier des Schrotts«. Der junge kalifornische Architekt legte in seinen bisherigen Bauten den Schwerpunkt vor allem auf ungewöhnliche Materialien. In seinen Entwürfen finden sich alte Ketten, gebrochene Balken und andere scheinbar deplazierte Elemente, die genauso auch zu einer modernen Skulptur passen könnten. Die bildenden Künste haben eine Freiheit erworben, die für die Architektur sowohl aufgrund der Durchführbarkeit und der Baubestimmungen als auch aufgrund der »Erwartungen« ihrer Klientel undenkbar schien. Eric Owen Moss sucht ebenso nach neuen Wegen, auf denen die Architektur »de-konstruiert« werden kann, wie der Österreicher Wolf Prix von Coop Himmelblau, der von Moss' Arbeiten begeistert ist. Sein Kennzeichen ist der intensive und experimentelle Umgang mit Materialien und Formen, wie man es in seinen Bauten in Culver City, Kalifornien, finden kann.

D'Eric Owen Moss (né en 1943) l'architecte Philip Johnson a écrit qu'il était «un orfèvre en ferraille». Dans son œuvre, ce jeune architecte californien a jusqu'à présent mis l'accent sur des matériaux inhabituels. Vieilles chaînes, poutres brisées et autres éléments incongrus trouvent leur place dans ses constructions, un peu comme dans une sculpture contemporaine. Les arts visuels ont acquis une liberté qui semblait interdite à l'architecture pour des contraintes de praticité et de réglementation de la construction, mais aussi du fait des «attentes» du public. Comme l'Autrichien Wolf Prix, principal responsable de Coop Himmelblau qui apprécie son travail, Eric Owen Moss explore actuellement les façons dont l'architecture peut être «déconstruite». Sa propre spécificité, évidente dans ses constructions de Culver City, en Californie, réside dans une expérimentation approfondie et inattendue des formes et des matériaux.

Gary Group, Culver City, California, 1988-90

A lot of this work is a social and political commentary on the world and the way it works.

Ein Großteil dieser Arbeiten ist ein sozialpolitischer Kommentar der Welt und ihrer Vorgänge.

Une grande partie de ce travail est un commentaire social et politique sur la façon dont va le monde.

ERIC OWEN MOSS

The floor plan shows the importance of the circular kitchen to the design. Windows on the side of the roof vault (left) give an impression of ongoing design adjustments.

Der Grundriß zeigt die Bedeutung der runden Küche für den Entwurf. Die Fenster auf der Seite des gewölbten Dachs (links) vermitteln einen Eindruck von den ständigen Änderungen des Projekts.

Le plan masse montre l'importance de la cuisine circulaire. Les fenêtres sur les côtés du toit voûté (à gauche) donnent une impression de «réglage» en cours de l'articulation des masses.

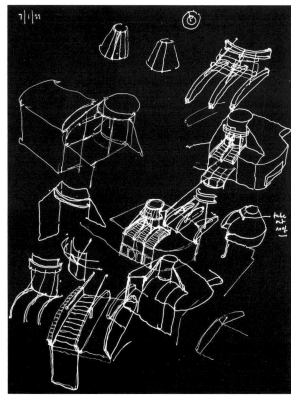

LAWSON/WESTEN HOUSE 1988-93
LOS ANGELES, CALIFORNIA

The clients live their lives around the kitchen, so that this space became the focal element of the building. Its drum-like shape, over 10 meters high, is completed by a sliced cone roof, with an ocean-view deck. Skylights and a vaulted roof are other features, with concrete and plaster for the exterior walls. The complex shape is marked by phases of the design process, an architectural equivalent of »pentimenti« in painting. The result is what the architect calls »incongruity and surprisingness«.

Da sich das Leben der Bewohner hauptsächlich um die Küche herum abspielt, wurde sie zum Zentrum. Ein Dach in Form eines angeschnittenen Kegels und eine Aussichtsplattform bilden den Abschluß dieses über zehn Meter hohen trommelförmigen Raums. Andere Merkmale sind die Oberlichter und das gewölbte Dach; die Außenwände bestehen aus Beton und Gips. Das Gebäude ist geprägt von den Entwurfsphasen und wirkt wie eine architektonische Entsprechung zu den »pentimenti« in der Malerei. Das Ergebnis bezeichnet Moss als »Unstimmigkeit und Überraschung«.

Les clients organisent leur vie autour de la cuisine, ce qui explique que cet espace est devenu l'élément central de cette maison. Sa forme de tambour, de plus de 10 m de haut, est complétée par un toit en forme de section de cône, avec point d'observation. Des verrières et un toit voûté figurent parmi les autres caractéristiques notables ainsi que des murs extérieurs en béton et en plâtre. La forme complexe garde les traces des phases du processus de création, équivalent architectural des «pentimenti» en peinture. Le résultat est ce que l'architecte appelle: «incongruité et surprise».

GARY GROUP 1988-90
CULVER CITY, CALIFORNIA

The Gary Group is part of a four build-ing complex with the Paramount Laundry and the Lindblade Tower. The architect calls the west façade the »mausoleum wall« because it includes new and old elements. Philip Johnson's name for Moss: »jeweler of junk« – the use of chains, re-bars and wheels proves his point. A tilted wall on the front of the building, the barred windows of the first floor and the empty ones of the second, give an im-pression of abandonment and collapse, despite the careful design.

Die Gary Group ist zusammen mit der Paramount Laundry und dem Lind-blade Tower Teil eines Komplexes aus vier Gebäuden. Der Architekt bezeich-net die Westfassade als »Mausoleums-wand«, da sie alte und neue Bauele-mente enthält. Philip Johnsons Be-zeichnung für Moss »Juwelier des Schrotts« erweist sich durch die Ver-wendung von Ketten, U-Bügeln und Rä-dern als treffend. Trotz des gut durch-dachten Entwurfs wirkt dieses Gebäu-de mit seiner schrägen Wand an der Vorderfront, den verbretterten Fen-stern im ersten Stock und den leeren Fenstern der zweiten Etage wie verlas-sen und dem Zusammenbruch nahe.

Le Gary Group fait partie d'un ensem-ble de quatre bâtiments comprenant la Paramount Laundry et la Lindblade Tower. L'architecte parle de la façade ouest comme du «mur du mausolée» parce qu'il comporte des éléments neufs et anciens. Philip Johnson quali-fie Moss «d'orfèvre en ferraille», ce que montre l'utilisation de chaînes, de barres et de roues. L'inclinaison du mur de façade, les fenêtres à barreaux du premier étage et les fenêtres vides du second donnent une impression de laisser-aller, voire même d'effondre-ment, en dépit du soin attentif porté à la conception générale.

The »mausoleum wall« (left page) is covered with re-bar »ladders« where plants will climb. The front façade is tilted back, and includes a clock, which is »perhaps legible«.

Die »Mausoleumswand« (linke Seite) ist mit »Leitern« aus U-Bügeln bedeckt, an denen Kletterpflanzen hochranken sollen. Die Vorderfront neigt sich nach hinten und trägt eine Uhr, die »vielleicht lesbar« ist.

Le «mur du mausolée», page de gauche, est recouvert de barreaux «d'échelle» où des plantes grimperont. La façade principale est inclinée vers l'arrière et comporte une horloge «peut-être lisible».

8522 NATIONAL BOULEVARD 1986-90
CULVER CITY, CALIFORNIA

Moss undertook a complete rehabilitation of five adjoining warehouses built between the 1920's and the 1940's. Because the buildings had no real entrance, he cut an elliptical entry court in from the street, leaving an exposed truss, breaking down barriers between interior and exterior. With a flexible disposition imposed by the unknown number of tenants, Moss combines existing structural elements with new spaces, such as the elliptical conference room.

Moss übernahm hier die Wiedereingliederung von fünf benachbarte Lagerhäusern von 1920 bis 1940. Als gemeinsamen Eingang fügte er auf der Straßenseite einen elliptischen Hof ein und ließ dort einen der Träger stehen. Er versuchte, die Schranken zwischen Innen und Außen zu durchbrechen. Da die Raumdisposition, bedingt durch die unbekannte Zahl der Mieter, flexibel sein mußte, kombinierte Moss Bestehendes mit Lösungen wie dem elliptischen Konferenzraum.

Moss a entrepris ici une réhabilitation de cinq entrepôts des entre les années vingt et quarante. Comme entrée, il a taillé une cour d'entrée elliptique, laissant la charpente apparente et manifestant ainsi son intérêt pour la suppression de la séparation dedans/dehors. Avec une implantation intérieure souple, due au fait qu'il ne savait pas qui allait occuper les lieux, Moss marie des éléments existants avec des espaces de nouveauté, comme une salle de conférence elliptique.

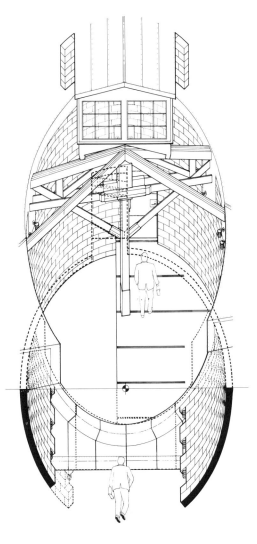

Both the entrance (left page: drawing), and the conference room (left page below) are elliptical in shape. Left open to the sky, the entrance area immediately leads the visitor to speculate on the relationships of old and new, inside and outside.

Sowohl der Eingang (linke Seite: Zeichnung) als auch der Konferenzraum (linke Seite unten) sind elliptisch in ihrer Grundform. Der nach oben offene Eingangsbereich regt den Besucher zum Nachdenken über Alt und Neu, Innen und Außen an.

L'entrée (page de gauche: dessin) et la salle de conférence (bas de la page de gauche) sont toutes deux elliptiques. A gauche, l'entrée à ciel ouvert interpelle le visiteur sur les relations entre l'ancien et le nouveau, le dedans et le dehors.

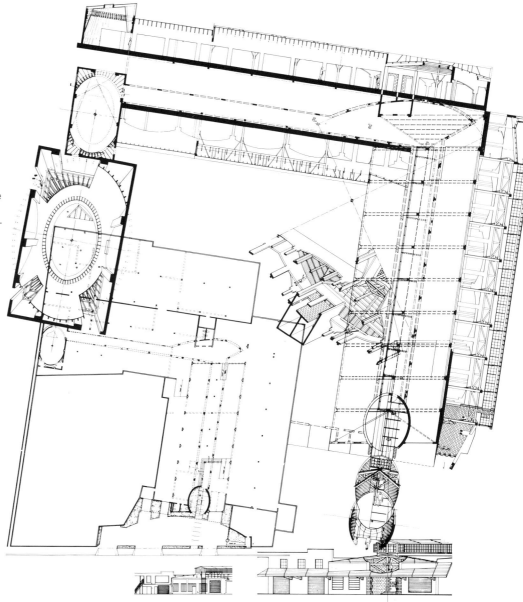

IEOH MING **PEI**

Ieoh Ming Pei (* 1917) has assumed the role of the elder statesman of American architecture. Influenced early in his career by Mies van der Rohe, he retains a conviction that Modernism, tempered with a respect for tradition which his Chinese origins have given him, remains a valid form of expression. Perhaps because of his association with the developer William Zeckendorf (1948-1960), Pei has not always had the favors of the architectural press, and difficult projects like the Hancock Tower in Boston (1966-76, designed by Henry Cobb), left his firm for long periods without much work. With the powerful geometry of the National Gallery's East Building (1968-78), or the Grand Louvre (1983-93), he has justified the citation of the jury of the 1983 Pritzker Prize: »I. M. Pei has given this century some of its most beautiful interior spaces and exterior forms.«

Ieoh Ming Pei (* 1917) hat die Rolle des »großen alten Mannes« der amerikanischen Architektur übernommen. Zu Beginn seiner Karriere durch Mies van der Rohe beeinflußt, hält er an der Überzeugung fest, daß die Moderne, wenn sie die Tradition respektiert, wie es ihn seine chinesische Herkunft lehrte, eine gültige Ausdrucksform bleibt. Vielleicht aufgrund seiner Zusammenarbeit mit dem Erfinder William Zeckendorf (1948-1960) fand Pei nicht immer das Lob der Architekturkritiker, und auch problematische Projekte wie der Hancock Tower in Boston (1966-76, entworfen von Henry Cobb) sorgten dafür, daß sein Büro lange Zeit ohne Aufträge blieb. Mit der ausdrucksvollen Geometrie des östlichen Anbaus der National Gallery (1968-78) oder dem Grand Louvre (1983-93) wurde er jedoch dem Lob der Jury des Pritzker Preises von 1983 gerecht: »I. M. Pei hat diesem Jahrhundert einige seiner schönsten Innenräume und Fassaden geschenkt.«

Ieoh Ming Pei (né en 1917) assume le rôle de doyen des grands maîtres de l'architecture américaine. Influencé au début de sa carrière par Mies van der Rohe, il conserve la conviction que le Modernisme, tempéré par un respect de la tradition dû à ses origines chinoises, reste une forme d'expression valable. Peut-être du fait de son association avec le promoteur William Zeckendorf (1948-60), Pei n'a pas toujours eu la faveur de la presse d'architecture et des projets difficiles comme la Hancock Tower de Boston (1966-76, dessinée par Henry Cobb) furent suivis de longues périodes d'activité ralentie. A travers la puissante composition géométrique de l'East Building de la National Gallery (1968-78), ou le Grand Louvre (1983-93), il a justifié le commentaire du jury du Prix Pritzker qu'il obtint en 1983: «I. M. Pei a apporté à ce siècle quelques-un de ses plus beaux espaces intérieurs et de ses plus belles formes extérieures.»

Bank of China Tower, Hong Kong, 1982-89

Geometry has always been the underpinning of my architecture.

Geometrie war immer schon das Fundament meiner Architektur.

La géométrie a toujours été le fondement de mon architecture.

I. M. PEI

It was François Mitterrand who person-
ally chose Pei as the architect for this
project, which was meant to give a
new coherence to the Louvre. The
master-plan, with its first phase cen-
tered around the pyramid, was designed to establish a clear pattern of
circulation to the underground parking
lots and to the Richelieu, Sully and
Denon wings. Pei likened the original
Louvre to a »theater without a back-
stage«, and the first phase included extensive underground storage areas as
well as large public spaces.

François Mitterrand persönlich wählte
Pei als Architekt für das Projekt der
Neugestaltung des Louvre aus. Der
Gesamtentwurf, in dessen erster Phase die Pyramide im Mittelpunkt steht,
will die unterirdischen Parkhäuser, den
Richelieu-, Sully- und den Denon-Flü-
gel miteinander verbinden. Pei vergleicht den ursprünglichen Louvre mit
einem »Theater ohne Kulissen«, bei
dem in der ersten Bauphase neben
großen unterirdischen Depots auch
Ausstellungsflächen entstehen sollen.

Ce fut François Mitterrand qui choisit
personnellement Pei pour ce projet,
destiné à donner une nouvelle cohé-
rence au Louvre. Le plan masse de la
première phase d'exécution centrée
autour de la pyramide établit un système clair de circulation vers les par-
kings, les ailes Richelieu, Sully et Denon. Pei compare le Louvre original à
un «théâtre sans coulisses» et la première phase comprenait de très vastes zones techniques souterraines ainsi que de grands espaces d'exposition.

I. M. Pei's renovation of the Louvre is one
of the most prestigious projects accomplished by an American architect in the late
20th century. To the right, the spiral stair-
case beneath the Pyramid.

I. M. Peis Renovierung des Louvre ist eines
der hervorragensten Projekte eines amerikanischen Architekten am Ende des 20. Jahrhunderts. Rechts: die Wendeltreppe unter-
halb der Pyramide.

La rénovation du Louvre par I. M. Pei est
l'un des plus prestigieux projets menés à
bien par un architecte américain en cette
fin du XXéme siècle. A droite, l'escalier en
spirale, sous la Pyramide.

Pei's plan called for the Pyramid to become the central entry for the Louvre. His inspiration was partly derived from the garden designer Le Nôtre, who emphasized sky and water as design elements.

Pei plante die Pyramide als Haupteingang für den Louvre. Er ließ sich teilweise vom Gartenarchitekten Le Nôtre inspirieren, der Himmel und Wasser als Gestaltungselemente hervorhob.

Les plans de Pei faisaient de la Pyramide, l'entrée principale du Louvre. Son inspiration vient, en partie, de l'œuvre de Le Nôtre, qui aimait se servir du ciel et de l'eau dans ses projets.

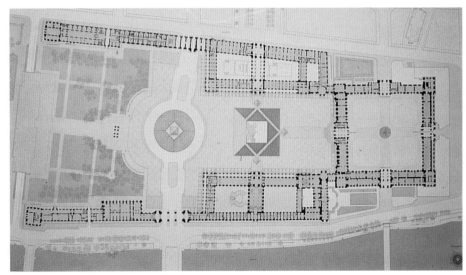

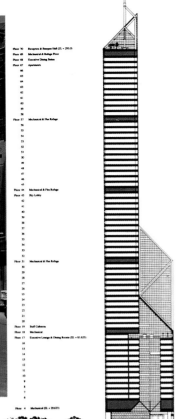

Building Section
North-South Section Looking West

0 ———— 26 M

The Bank of China Tower is close to Norman Foster's Hong Kong and Shanghai Bank building. Pei's building rests on a tone base, and is partially surrounded by a rock garden.

Der Bank of China Tower steht in der Nähe von Norman Fosters Gebäude der Hong Kong and China Bank. Peis Gebäude besitzt einen steinernen Sockel und ist teilweise von einem Steingarten umgeben.

La tour de la Banque de Chine est proche du bâtiment construit par Norman Foster pour la Banque de Hong Kong & de Shangaï. Elle repose sur un socle de pierre, partiellement entouré d'un jardin de rocaille.

BANK OF CHINA TOWER 1982-89
HONG KONG

Located on a small, difficult site, the Bank of China building rises 70 stories. As in Washington's East Building for the National Gallery, the Bank of China Tower is based on a triangular geometry, translated here in an innovative structural system, which permitted the building to meet Hong Kong's tough typhoon-influenced code, while minimizing the use of steel. Although criticized as a symbol of main-land dominance, it gives the chaotic urban pattern of the city a clear point of focus.

Das 70 Stockwerke hohe Gebäude der Bank of China steht auf einem kleinen, problematischen Grundstück. Wie der Ostflügel der National Gallery in Washington basiert der Turm auf einem Dreieck. Mit Hilfe einer neuen Bautechnik konnte trotz der Hongkonger Taifun-Verordnungen die Verwendung von Stahl minimiert werden. Der Turm verleiht dem städtischen Gewirr einen klaren Bezugspunkt, auch wenn er als Symbol der chinesischen Vormachtstellung kritisiert wurde.

Edifié sur un site étroit et difficile, l'immeuble de la Banque de Chine compte 70 étages. Comme dans l'East Building de la National Gallery de Washington, la construction part d'une géométrie triangulaire, transférée ici dans un système structurant qui répond aux exigences de la réglementation anti-typhons de Hong Kong tout en réduisant l'utilisation de l'acier. Bien que critiquée pour être le symbole de la domination de la Chine, elle offre au paysage urbain un point de focalisation.

MORTON H. MEYERSON SYMPHONY CENTER 1981-89
DALLAS, TEXAS

With the actual concert hall rotated off of the axes of the street grid to face the downtown area, the Meyerson Symphony Center demonstrates the same elegant simplicity as all of Pei's major projects. An unusual feature here is the inclusion of three curved skylights, whose complex pattern is echoed in the lobby. Although Pei is decidedly not a historicist, in describing his lobby design he has made reference to Balthasar Neumann (1687-1753), and to the grand staircase of Charles Garnier's Paris Opera.

Die Konzerthalle wurde aus der Achse des Straßenrasters gerückt und blickt in Richtung Innenstadt. Das Meyerson Symphony Center hat die gleiche elegante Schlichtheit wie alle Großprojekte Peis. Ungewöhnlich sind die drei gebogenen Oberlichter, deren komplizierter Schnitt sich in der Lobby wiederholt. Obwohl Pei nicht zu den Historisten zählt, bezieht er sich bei der Beschreibung der Lobby auf Balthasar Neumann (1687-1753) und auf Charles Garniers Treppenhaus der Pariser Oper.

En faisant pivoter la salle de concert par rapport aux axes de la trame de la voirie pour faire face au centre de la ville, le Meyerson Symphony Center fait preuve d'une simplicité comme tous les autres grands projets de Pei. Inhabituel est cependant ici l'inclusion de trois verrières inclinées dont le dessin complexe se retrouve dans le hall d'accueil. Bien que Pei ne soit absolument pas un historiciste, il a fait référence à Balthasar Neumann (1687-1753) et à l'escalier de l'Opéra de Paris de Charles Garnier.

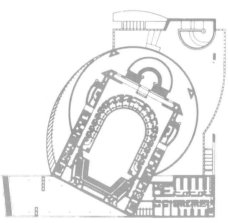

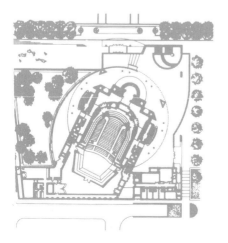

Pei calls the curved skylights »lenses«. Their shape has a clear relationship to the spectacular entrance spaces. Left page: the nearly circular »Dedication Wall«.

Pei nennt die gerundeten Oberlichter »Linsen«. Ihre Form bildet einen deutlichen Bezug zum spektakulären Eingangsbereich. Linke Seite: die nahezu kreisrunde »Dedication Wall« (Wand der Widmungen).

Pei parle de «lentilles» pour ces verrières incurvées. Leur forme assume une relation claire avec les spectaculaires volumes de l'entrée. Page de gauche, le «Mur des dédicaces» presque circulaire.

SHINJI SHUMEKAI BELL TOWER 1988-90
MISONO, SHIGA, JAPAN

Just over 65 meters high, this simple, dramatic structure was built for a religious sect on a mountainous site near Kyoto. It is in a complex whose center is a sanctuary designed by Minoru Yamasaki, the architect of New York's World Trade Center. The tower is clad in a pale Vermont granite, and its shape was inspired by the »bachi«, which is used to pluck the strings of a traditional Japanese instrument. In its strong design, the structure is typical of Pei's late work.

Der schlichte und doch beeindruckende Turm für eine religiöse Sekte ist knapp über 65 Meter hoch und steht vor einem Gebirgsmassiv, nicht weit von Kyoto. Er gehört zu einem Komplex, der sich um ein Heiligtum gruppiert, das von Minoru Yamasaki entworfen wurde, dem Architekten des World Trade Center in New York. Der Turm ist mit hellem Granit aus Vermont verkleidet. Seine Form wurde durch die »bachi« angeregt, die dazu benutzt werden, die Saiten eines traditionellen japanischen Instruments zu zupfen. Der energische Entwurf ist typisch für I. M. Peis Spätwerk.

Mesurant un peu plus de 65 m de haut, cette structure simple et dramatique a été construite dans un site montagneux non loin de Kyoto, pour une secte religieuse. Elle est située dans un ensemble dont le centre est un sanctuaire dessiné par Minoru Yamasaki, l'architecte du World Trade Center de New York. La tour est recouverte d'un granit du Vermont très pâle et sa forme a été inspirée par le «bachi» utilisé pour pincer les cordes d'un instrument de musique traditionnel japonais. Sa forme puissante est caractéristique des œuvres récentes d' I. M. Pei.

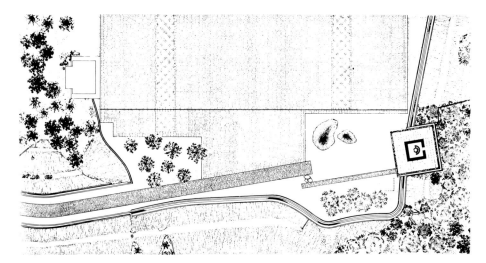

Visitors discover the Bell Tower by walking up a curved forest path paved with old Kyoto stones. Used for religious functions, the space at the base of the tower is consecrated, like that of a temple.

Am Ende eines gewundenen Waldweges, der mit Steinen aus dem alten Kyoto gepflastert ist, ragt der Glockenturm vor den Besuchern auf. Der Bereich am Fuß des Turmes wird für religiöse Zwecke genutzt und gilt daher als geweihter Boden.

Les visiteurs découvrent le campanile en empruntant un sentier forestier recouvert d'anciens pavés de Kyoto. Consacré comme un temple, l'espace à la base de la tour est utilisé à des fonctions religieuses.

ANTOINE **PREDOCK**

Although Antoine Predock (* 1936) rejects the notion that he is an »adobe architect«, it is clear that there are references in his work to the tradition of the south-western United States. Based in Albuquerque, New Mexico, he often designs blunt, windowless forms which bring to mind the mud architecture which existed in the region long before the arrival of the Spanish, but also recall some of Frank Lloyd Wright's work. The muted, earthen colors he employs also seem typical of a desert climate, although he has made a point of abandoning these colors when he works in California. In this sense, his principal source is much more »native« American than modern, and yet he has proven, through his residences and larger buildings that he is capable of generating a new vocabulary, which may become very influential.

Obwohl es Antoine Predock (* 1936) ablehnt, als »Adobe«-Architekt bezeichnet zu werden, bestehen offensichtliche Beziehungen zwischen seinen Arbeiten und der Bautradition des Südwestens der USA. In seinem Büro in Albuquerque, New Mexico, entwirft er häufig schlichte fensterlose Gebäudeformen, die nicht nur an die Lehmbauten der Umgebung erinnern, die hier schon lange vor der Ankunft der Spanier existierten, sondern auch an einzelne Bauten von Frank Lloyd Wright. Auch die gedämpften irdenen Farben, die er verwendet, scheinen typisch für das Wüstenklima. Wenn Predock jedoch Bauten für kalifornische Auftraggeber entwirft, arbeitet er mit völlig anderen Farben. Insgesamt sind seine Entwürfe eher von den Ureinwohnern Amerikas als von der Moderne beeinflußt. Predock hat durch Einfamilienhäuser und größere Gebäudekomplexe gezeigt, daß er dazu fähig ist, ein neues Vokabular zu entwickeln, das eines Tages vielleicht von großem Einfluß sein wird.

Bien qu'Antoine Predock (né en 1936) rejette le qualificatif d'«architecte de l'adobe», les références à la tradition du sud-ouest américain sont très présentes dans son œuvre. Installé à Albuquerque, Nouveau Mexique, il dessine souvent des formes dépouillées, sans fenêtre, qui font penser à l'architecture de terre qui existait dans cette région bien avant l'arrivée des Espagnols, mais également à certaines œuvres de Frank Lloyd Wright. Les couleurs terreuses, atténuées, qu'il emploie sont également typiques du désert bien qu'il se soit efforcé d'abandonner ces coloris lorsqu'il a travaillé en Californie, par exemple. Sa principale source d'inspiration semble donc plus «indigène» américaine que moderne même s'il a prouvé, pour des résidences privées ou de plus importants projets qu'il était capable de créer un vocabulaire nouveau susceptible d'exercer une grande influence.

Hotel Santa Fe, Euro Disney, Marne-la-Vallée, France, 1992

My basic approach to design is to be site-specific – expressing spirit of place.

Die Grundlage meiner Entwürfe ist immer der Ort – der Ausdruck des Geistes eines Ortes.

Mon approche de base est d'être spécifique au site, d'exprimer l'esprit du lieu.

ANTOINE PREDOCK

ZUBER HOUSE 1986-89
PHOENIX, ARIZONA

Set against a mountain, this house re-calls regional architecture because of its flat, unadorned façades. Its L-shaped plan, however, with east-west and north-south oriented elements, together with the unexpected angled »bridge«, make it clear that Antoine Predock is not imitating the »adobe« style. The bridge is a viewing platform, which crosses over the entrance, form-ing a gate. In this arid environment, water enters the house via a waterfall and interior »silent pool«.

Vor dem Hintergrund der Berge erin-nert das Haus mit seinen glatten, schmucklosen Fassaden an die Archi-tektur der Region. Trotzdem macht der L-förmige Grundriß mit Baukörpern in Ost-West- und Nord-Süd-Ausrichtung und einer davon abweichenden Brük-ke deutlich, daß Predock nicht den »Adobe«-Stil imitiert. Die Brücke ist eine Aussichtsplattform, die über den Eingang führt und so ein Tor formt. In dieser trockenen Landschaft wird Was-ser über einen Wasserfall und einen in-neren »stillen Teich« ins Haus geleitet.

Au pied d'une montagne, cette mai-son rappelle, avec son toit plat et ses façade nues, l'architecture régionale. Cependant, son plan en L, ses orienta-tions est-ouest et nord-sud, et le «pont» inattendu montrent à l'éviden-ce que Predock ne cherche pas à expri-mer le style «adobe». Le pont est réel-lement une plate-forme d'observation, qui passe au-dessus de l'entrée et for-me un portail. Dans cet environne-ment aride, l'eau pénètre la maison par une chute d'eau et un bassin inté-rieur.

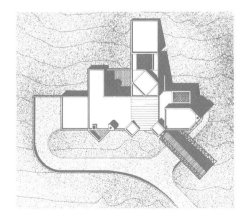

A rather forbidding exterior, almost fortress-like in its strong lines, gives way to a luminous interior which is rendered even more hospitable by the presence of fresh, running water.

Ein abschreckendes Äußeres, festungsähnlich in seiner strengen Linienführung, öffnet sich in ein strahlendes Inneres, das durch das frische Wasser gastlich wirkt.

Un extérieur assez rebutant, dont les lignes puissantes font presque penser à une forteresse, dissimule un intérieur lumineux rendu encore plus hospitalier par la présence d'eau vive.

As in most of his buildings, Antoine Predock makes extensive use of the play of strong light and shadow by orchestrating numerous small openings. A horizontal view looks like a city-scape.

Wie bei den meisten seiner Bauten spielt Antoine Predock auch hier ausgiebig mit Licht und Schatten, indem er bewußt zahlreiche kleine Fensteröffnungen setzte. Die Ansicht ähnelt einer Stadtlandschaft.

Comme dans la plupart de ses constructions, Antoine Predock utilise abondamment le jeu de l'ombre et de la lumière grâce à de nombreuses petites ouvertures. En vision horizontale on pourrait presque penser à un paysage urbain.

NELSON FINE ARTS CENTER 1986-89
ARIZONA STATE UNIVERSITY, TEMPE, ARIZONA

A museum, dance and theater studios, and a 500 seat performance facility form the basic public space of this focal point for the campus of Arizona State University. Since it is divided into sections, the Education Building, Lecture Hall, Music Center, Theater, and Museum, the whole gives an impression of forming a desert city skyline. Although the layout of the complex is quite rational, the exterior brings to mind an image of almost haphazard, natural urban growth.

Ein Museum, verschiedene Tanz- und Theaterstudios sowie einen Veranstaltungssaal mit 500 Sitzen bilden das Zentrum auf dem Campus der Arizona State University. Da das Projekt in einzelne Bereiche unterteilt ist – Ausbildungsgebäude, Vorlesungssäle, Musikzentrum, Theater und Museum – erinnert der Komplex an die Skyline einer Wüstenstadt. Trotz rationaler Planung entsteht der Eindruck natürlichen städtischen Wachstums.

Un musée, des studios de danse et de théâtre et une salle de spectacle de 500 places trouvent place au centre du campus d'Arizona State University. Divisé en sections, Bâtiment de l'Education, Salle de conférences, Salle de concert, Théâtre et Musée, l'ensemble, fait penser à une ville du désert. Bien que le plan général soit assez rationnel, l'extérieur donne une impression de hasard ou de croissance urbaine naturelle.

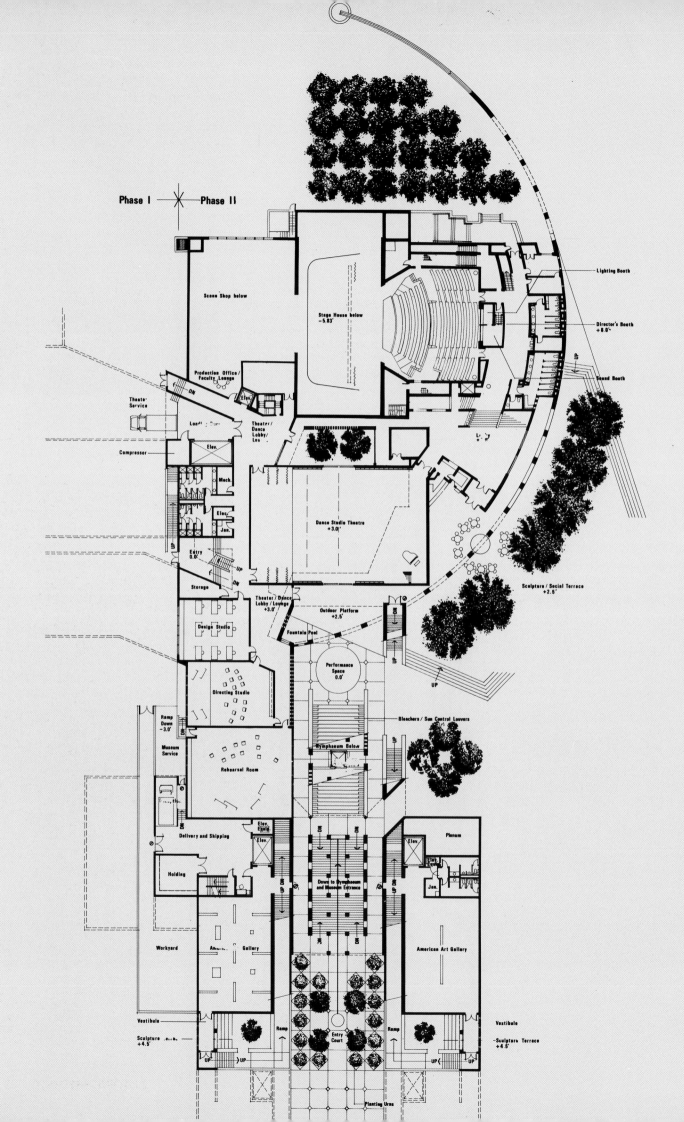

Phase I ──╳── Phase II

Scene Shop below

Stage House below
−5.83'

Lighting Booth

Director's Booth
+8.0'

Sound Booth

Production Office /
Faculty Lounge

Theater
Service

Loading Dock

Theater /
Dance
Lobby / Lou

Elev.

Compressor

Elev.

Mech.

Elec.

Jan.

UP

Entry
0.0'

UP

DN

Storage

Design Studio

Theater / Dance
Lobby / Lounge
+3.0'

Fountain Pool

Outdoor Platform
+2.5'

Dance Studio Theatre
+3.0'

Lobby
+3.0'

Sculpture / Social Terrace
+2.5'

DN

UP

Performance
Space
0.0'

UP

Directing Studio

Ramp
Down
−3.0'

Museum
Service

Bleachers / Sun Control Louvers

Rehearsal Room

Nymphaeum Below

Delivery and Shipping

Elev. Child.

Elev.

DN

DN

Holding

DN

Down to Nymphaeum
and Museum Entrance

Plenum

Elev.

Elev.

Jan.

Workyard

American Art Gallery

American Art Gallery

Vestibule

Vestibule

Sculpture Terrace
+4.5'

Ramp

Entry
Court

Ramp

UP

UP

Sculpture Terrace
+4.5'

UP

UP

Planting Urns

The carefully arranged floor plan gives way, in the juxtaposition of the varied roof elements, to an impression of extreme, almost organic complexity, dominated by local colors.

Der sorgfältig durchdachte Grundriß steht in einem Wechselspiel mit den verschiedenen Dachformen und vermittelt dem Betrachter einen Eindruck der extremen, fast organischen Komplexität, die von den für die Gegend typischen Farben beherrscht wird.

A travers la juxtaposition des éléments de toiture, l'axonométrie donne une impression de complexité, presque organique, soulignée par les couleurs locales.

The vocabulary of geometric forms is juxtaposed by Predock in unexpected patterns, as evidenced in the large square opening of the triangular Administration block.

Das Vokabular geometrischer Formen ist von Predock zu überraschenden Mustern verarbeitet worden, wie sich in der großen quadratischen Öffnung des dreieckigen Verwaltungsgebäudes zeigt.

Predock joue ici d'un vocabulaire inattendu de formes géométriques et de compositions inhabituelles, comme le montre la grande ouverture carrée du bloc de l'administration triangulaire.

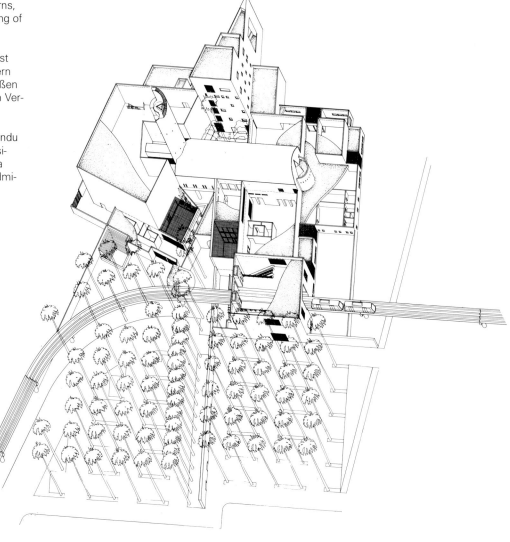

LAS VEGAS LIBRARY AND MUSEUM 1987-90
LAS VEGAS, NEVADA

Antoine Predock would not seem to have been greatly influenced by Venturi's »Learning from Las Vegas«. His »desert building« has strong, simple forms, which reach their highest point in the 35 meter high »Science Tower«, whose upper curves resemble certain Indian observatories. The 10,000 square meter building relies on state-of-the-art technology in both the Young People's Library and the Discovery Museum, which deals with transportation, energy, and the principles of science and mathematics.

Antoine Predock scheint eigentlich von Robert Venturis Buch »Learning from Las Vegas« nicht besonders beeinflußt worden zu sein. Sein »Wüstenhaus« besitzt starke, einfache Formen, die in einem 35 Meter hohen »Wissenschaftsturm« enden, dessen Abschlußrundung an indianische Observatorien erinnert. In dem 10 000 m² großen Gebäudekomplex liegen sowohl die Young People's Library als auch das Discovery Museum, das sich mit Transportwesen, Energie und den Grundlagen von Wissenschaft und Mathematik befaßt; beide sind mit modernster Technik ausgestattet.

Antoine Predock n'a pas été très influencé par le livre de Venturi «Learning from Las Vegas». Son «bâtiment du désert» possède des formes puissantes et simples qui atteignent leur plus haute expression dans la «Tour de la science» de 35 m de haut, laquelle rappelle certains observatoires indiens. Le bâtiment de 10 000 mètres carrés fait appel à une technologie d'avant-garde à la fois dans la Bibliothèque des Jeunes, et le Discovery Museum consacré au transport, à l'énergie, aux sciences et aux mathématiques.

BART PRINCE

Bart Prince (* 1947) may not be one of the best-known architects in the United States, but his work, which is resolutely situated outside of the current mainstream, carries on a strong tradition, which includes certain buildings by Frank Lloyd Wright, and the »oeuvre« of Bruce Goff. Bart Prince worked extensively with Bruce Goff, beginning in 1970, and like Goff, his buildings project a strong sense of craftsmanship and a close relationship to natural forms. The pure lines of Modernism could not be further from his mind, but Prince's inventiveness recalls not only the pioneering force of Wright, but also that of Gaudí. A native of the southwest, he has not indulged in the references to »native« architecture that have been the focus of the work of Antoine Predock, for example.

Bart Prince (* 1947) zählt nicht gerade zu den bekanntesten Architekten der USA, aber seine Arbeiten, die außerhalb gängiger Trends liegen, orientieren sich an einer Tradition, die sowohl einzelne Bauten von Frank Lloyd Wright als auch das »Oeuvre« von Bruce Goff einschließt. Seit 1970 arbeitete Bart Prince intensiv mit Goff zusammen, und genau wie dessen Bauten zeigen die von Prince handwerkliches Können und eine enge Beziehung zu natürlichen Formen. Nichts liegt ihm ferner als die geraden Linien der Moderne, aber Prince' Erfindungsgabe weckt nicht nur die Erinnerung an die bahnbrechende Kraft eines Wright, sondern auch an die eines Gaudí. Im Gegensatz zu Antoine Predock finden sich in seinem Werk keine Einflüsse der ursprünglichen Architektur der Region, obwohl auch er im Südwesten der USA geboren wurde.

Né en 1947, Bart Prince n'est peut-être pas le plus connu des architectes américains, mais son œuvre, qui se situe résolument en dehors des principaux courants, se nourrit d'une forte tradition qui comprend certains édifices de Frank Lloyd Wright et l'œuvre de Bruce Goff. Dès 1970, Bart Prince a beaucoup travaillé avec ce dernier et, comme chez Goff, ses constructions traduisent un sens marqué du savoir-faire artisanal et une relation étroite avec les formes naturelles. Rien n'est plus éloigné de son esprit que les lignes pures du Modernisme. Sa créativité rappelle à la fois les recherches d'avant-garde de Wright et celles de Gaudí. Né dans le Sud-Ouest, il ne se complaît pas dans les références à l'architecture indigène qui figurent au centre des travaux d'Antoine Predock, par exemple.

Joe and Etsuko Price Residence, Corona del Mar, California, 1983-90

The forms do not determine spaces ... the spaces and their functions determine the forms.

Nicht die Formen bestimmen den Raum ... der Raum und seine Funktionen bestimmen die Form.

Les formes ne déterminent pas les espaces ... les espaces et leurs fonctions déterminent les formes.

BART PRINCE

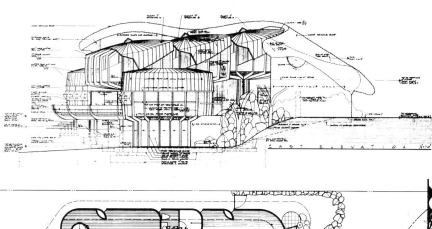

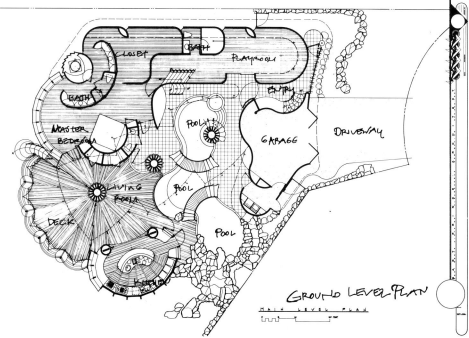

GROUND LEVEL PLAN

MAIN LEVEL PLAN

Laminated wood surfaces are used both in-side and out, showing as Bart Prince says, that »the entire design grew from the in-side, out«. A floor plan shows the sinuous central pool.

Innen und außen wurde laminiertes Holz verwendet, das verdeutlicht, wie »der ge-samte Entwurf von innen nach außen wuchs«, wie Bart Prince sagt. Ein Grundriß zeigt den geschwungenen zentralen Pool.

Le bois contreplaqué est utilisé à l'intérieur comme à l'extérieur, illustrant le propos de Prince selon lequel «toute la conception a grandi de l'intérieur vers l'extérieur». Le plan masse montre la piscine centrale si-nueuse.

JOE AND ETSUKO PRICE
RESIDENCE 1983-90
CORONA DEL MAR, CALIFORNIA

It is not only a coincidence that this client's father was involved with Frank Lloyd Wright, and that Joe Price asked Bruce Goff to build a previous house. These figures represent the current that Bart Prince now leads, as exemplified in this house, built around a central courtyard and swimming pool. Stressing the importance of craftsmanship, the Price residence demonstrates the architect's overall concept, extending to the interior, as well as the »organic« exterior.

Es ist sicherlich kein Zufall, daß der Vater von Joe Price mit Frank Lloyd Wright in Verbindung stand und daß Price selbst für sein früheres Haus Bruce Goff als Architekten engagierte. Beide Baumeister vertraten eine stilistische Richtung, die heute von Bart Prince angeführt wird und die sich in diesem Haus spiegelt, das um einen zentralen Innenhof und einen Pool gebaut wurde. Die Price Residence betont die Bedeutung handwerklichen Könnens und steht stellvertretend für das Gesamtkonzept des Architekten sowohl im Inneren als auch im »organischen« Äußeren.

Ce n'est pas une pure coïncidence si le père de son client connaissait Frank Lloyd Wright et si Joe Price avait demandé à Bruce Goff de lui construire sa précédente maison. Ces grands architectes représentent en effet le courant dont Bart Prince a pris la tête, comme le montre cette maison, construite autour d'une cour centrale et d'une piscine. Mettant l'accent sur le savoir-faire artisanal, la résidence Price met en valeur le concept global de l'architecte, s'étendant à l'intérieur comme à l'extérieur «organique».

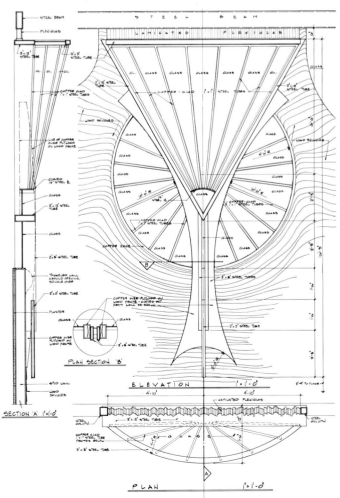

SITE

Although unusual in its conception, the Site group has consistently offered an alternative vision of contemporary architecture since it was founded in 1970. The principals of the firm, James Wines and Alison Sky, were not trained as architects, but rather as artists, and their projects have consistently challenged the uniformity of the built environment. Before the idea of »deconstructivist« architecture had taken firm hold, James Wines wrote a book entitled »De-Architecture« (1987) which made parallels between buildings and works of art like those of Christo or Robert Smithson, and challenged the idea that architecture must assume set forms. Site has also been at the forefront of the recent interest in environmentally concerned architecture, and early projects like the Highrise of Homes (1982), proposed bringing nature into the urban environment.

Seit der Gründung 1970 hat die in ihrer Konzeption ungewöhnliche Gruppe Site eine durchweg alternative Sicht zeitgenössischer Architektur geboten. Die Leiter der Gruppe, James Wines und Alison Sky, sind keine ausgebildeten Architekten, sondern Künstler. Ihre Projekte bilden eine ständige Herausforderung an die Uniformität der bebauten Umgebung. Bevor sich der Begriff der dekonstruktivistischen Architektur durchgesetzt hatte, schrieb James Wines 1987 sein Buch »De-Architecture«, in dem er Parallelen zwischen Bau- und Kunstwerken, wie denen von Robert Smithson oder Christo zieht. Er verwirft darin den Gedanken, daß Architektur fest umrissene Formen haben sollte. Site ist einer der Vorkämpfer einer umweltbewußten Architektur, und versuchte schon in frühen Projekten, wie dem Highrise of Homes (1982), die Natur in eine urbane Umgebung einzubeziehen.

Peu commun dans ses conceptions, le groupe Site a proposé avec constance, depuis sa création en 1970, une vision alternative de l'architecture contemporaine. Les responsables du groupe, James Wines et Alison Sky, ont reçu une formation plus artistique qu'architecturale et leurs projets remettent en permanence en cause l'uniformité de l'environnement construit. Avant que l'idée du «déconstructivisme» ait vraiment fait son apparition, James Wines avait écrit un livre intitulé «De-Architecture» (1987) qui traçait des parallèles entre des bâtiments et des œuvres d'art comme celles de Christo ou de Robert Smithson et s'opposait à l'idée que l'architecture doive revêtir des formes déterminées. Site s'est également trouvé à l'avant-garde d'une tendance de l'architecture soucieuse de l'environnement et des projets déjà anciens, comme le Highrise of Homes (1982), proposaient de faire entrer la nature dans l'environnement urbain.

Japan Cultural Center, Paris, France, project, 1990

This period began as the Age of Information, but it is becoming the Age of Ecology.

Diese Periode begann als Zeitalter der Information und entwickelt sich zum Zeitalter der Ökologie.

Alors que cette période a commencé comme l'âge de l'information, elle devient l'âge de l'écologie.

JAMES WINES

AVENUE 5 1992
WORLD EXPO, SEVILLE, SPAIN

Site was called on to design one of the five main pedestrian corridors on the Cartuja island, leading to the national pavilions. Using the theme of water, suggested by the proximity of the Guadalquivir river, they built a 300 meter long, undulating wall of glass, which was covered with flowing water, enclosing restaurant facilities and a monorail station. As in other recent projects, Site gave considerable importance to vegetation, including a vine-covered trellis, and many trees.

Site wurde beauftragt, einen der fünf Hauptzugangswege für Fußgänger auf der Insel Cartuja zu entwerfen, die zu den Länder-Pavillons führten. Die Nähe des Flusses Guadalquivir regte die Gruppe dazu an, diesem Projekt das Thema »Wasser« zugrunde zu legen. Site baute einen 300 Meter langen, wellenförmigen Glaswall mit Restaurants und dem Bahnhof für eine Einschienenbahn, der von fließendem Wasser überspült wurde. Wie in anderen kürzlich erstellten Projekten legte Site besonderen Wert auf die Begrünung des Projekts; in diesem Falle verwendete man Spaliere mit Weinranken und zahlreiche Bäume.

Site a été choisi pour dessiner l'une des cinq avenues piétonnes principales desservant les pavillons nationaux sur l'île de la Cartuja. S'inspirant du thème de l'eau, suggéré par la proximité du Guadalquivir, le groupe a construit un mur de verre de forme ondulée de 300 m de long, sur lequel coulait en permanence de l'eau et qui abritait des restaurants et une gare de monorail. Comme dans d'autres projets, Site a donné une importance considérable à la végétation (treille couverte de vigne et nombreux arbres).

Waterwall, promenade, and restaurant

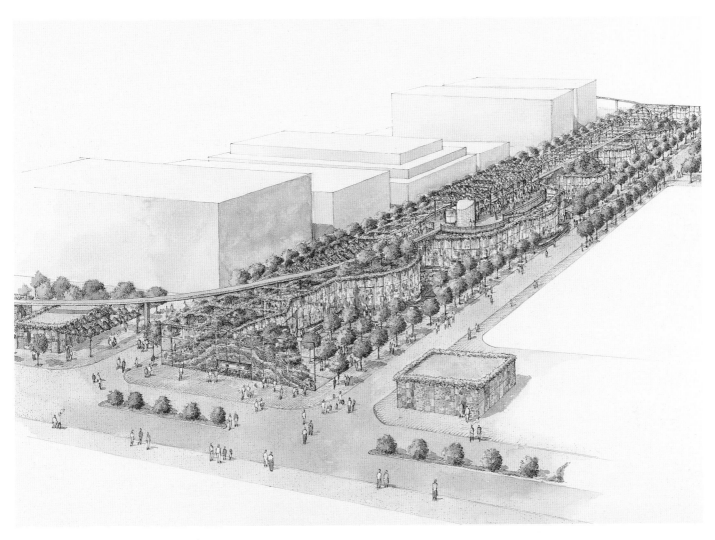

The Guadalquivir river flowing around the exhibition site was the thematic and historical point of departure for Site's project, together with the insistence on ecology which characterizes the group.

Der Guadalquivir, der das Gelände umfließt, war der thematische und historische Ausgangspunkt für Site's Projekt. Charakteristisch für diese Gruppe ist die bewußte Integration der Natur in den Entwurf.

Le Guadalquivir qui coule autour du site de l'Exposition servit de point de départ thématique et historique au projet de Site. L'attention donnée aux préoccupations écologiques est trés caractéristique de ce groupe d'architectes.

The fan-shaped design evokes the rising sun and its rays. The roof structures are intended to be covered with vegetation, which should facilitate heating in winter and cooling in summer.

Der fächerförmige Entwurf erinnert an die aufgehende Sonne und ihre Strahlen. Die Dächer sollen begrünt werden, um das Heizen im Winter und die Kühlung im Sommer zu erleichtern.

Le dessin en éventail évoque le lever du soleil et ses rayons. Les structures des toits doivent dans le temps se recouvrir de végétation, ce qui devrait faciliter le chauffage en hiver et la climatisation en été.

SHINWA RESORT (PROJECT) 1991
KISOKOMA-KOGEN, JAPAN

Situated in a mountainous area whose topography is suited to the fan-shaped design, the Shinwa Resort is a recent expression of the on-going interest of James Wines and Site in the integration of architecture and nature. An 8,000 square meter resort and 15,000 square meter hotel are intended to »grow organically« out of the environment. In response to the traditional ambiguity of Japanese architecture, »inside« and »outside« become relative concepts with vegetation present both within and without.

Das Shinwa Resort zeigt das ungebrochene Interesse von James Wines und Site, die Integration der Architektur in die Natur voranzutreiben. Das Projekt liegt in einem bergigen Gebiet, dessen Topographie sich dem fächerförmigen Muster anpaßt. Ein 8000 m^2 großes Erholungsgebiet und ein 15 000 m^2 großes Hotel sollen »organisch« aus dem Gelände erwachsen. »Innen« und »Außen« werden zu relativen Begriffen, da hier wie dort die Vegetation gedeiht und so die traditionelle Doppeldeutigkeit japanischer Architektur spiegelt.

Situés dans une zone montagneuse, le Shinwa Resort et sa forme en éventail sont bien adaptés à la topographie et témoignent de l'intérêt que James Wines et Site portent depuis longtemps à l'intégration nature/architecture. Ce centre de loisirs de 8000 mètres carrés et l'hôtel de 15000 mètres carrés sont supposés avoir «poussé» dans leur environnement. Comme en écho à l'ambiguïté traditionnelle de l'architecture japonaise, et avec une végétation présente aussi bien à l'intérieur qu'à l'extérieur, le «dedans» et le «dehors» deviennent ici des concepts relatifs.

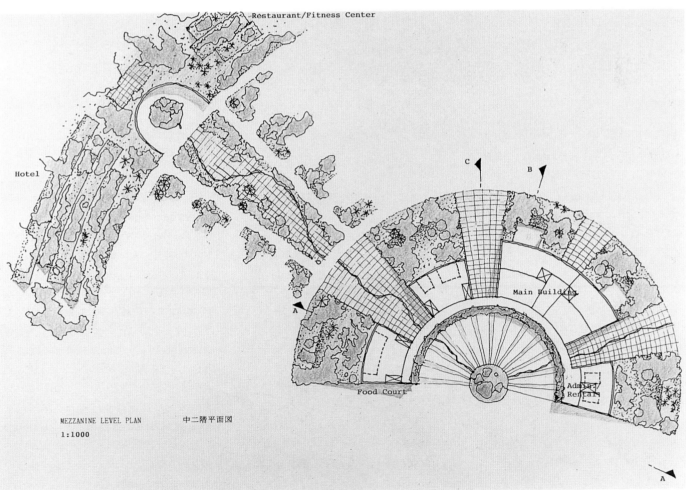

Restaurant/Fitness Center

Hotel

C B

Main Building

A

Food Court

Admin./
Rentals

A

MEZZANINE LEVEL PLAN 中二階平面図
1:1000

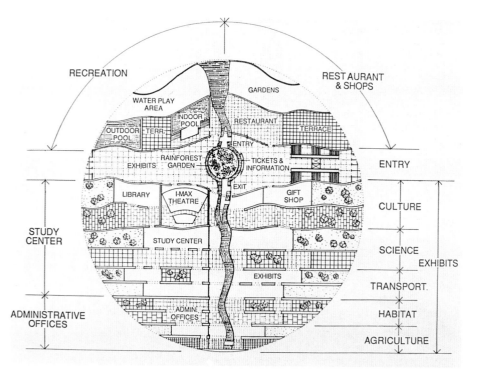

RECREATION

GARDENS

RESTAURANT & SHOPS

WATER PLAY AREA

INDOOR POOL

OUTDOOR POOL

TERR.

RESTAURANT

TERRACE

ENTRY

ENTRY

RAINFOREST GARDEN

EXHIBITS

TICKETS & INFORMATION

CULTURE

EXIT

LIBRARY

I-MAX THEATRE

GIFT SHOP

SCIENCE

EXHIBITS

STUDY CENTER

STUDY CENTER

EXHIBITS

TRANSPORT.

ADMINISTRATIVE OFFICES

ADMIN. OFFICES

HABITAT

AGRICULTURE

TENNESSEE RIVER

RIVERFRONT PARKWAY

MAIN ENTRANCE

SECOND STREET

SERVICE

THIRD STREET

SITE PLAN

TENNESSEE AQUA CENTER (PROJECT) 1993
CHATTANOOGA, TENNESSEE

In line with the city's desire to become a »leading environmental center«, this project is a museum dedicated to demonstrating the value of water in the development of civilization. Under a domed skylight in the entry hall, there will be an enclosed rainforest garden. Around it, there will be an Imax theater, a library, gift shop, study center, restaurant, pools and exhibits. The main area is a 183 meter diameter circle enclosing 14,000 square meters of interior space and as much exterior space.

Dieses Projekt soll die Bedeutung von Wasser in der Entwicklung der Zivilisation demonstrieren und entsteht in Übereinstimmung mit den Bemühungen der Stadt Chattanooga, zu »einem der führenden Umweltzentren« zu werden. Unter einem kuppelförmigen Oberlicht in der Eingangshalle soll ein tropischer Garten heranwachsen, um den herum ein Imax-Kino, eine Bibliothek, ein Souvenirladen, ein Arbeitszentrum, ein Restaurant, Pools und Ausstellungen geplant sind. Den Kernbereich bildet ein Kreis von 183 Metern Durchmesser mit 14 000 m² Innen- und ebensoviel Außenraum.

Dans le cadre des ambitions de la ville de devenir un «centre majeur pour l'environnement», ce projet est celui d'un musée consacré à la valeur de l'eau dans le développement de la civilisation. Sous le dôme en verrière du hall d'entrée se trouvera un jardin-forêt vierge. Autour s'articuleront une salle de cinéma Imax, une bibliothèque, une boutique de cadeaux, un centre d'études, un restaurant, des bassins et des galeries d'exposition. La zone principale est un cercle de 183 m de diamètre contenant 14 000 mètres carrés d'espace intérieur et autant d'espace en plein air.

The Aqua Center is intended to be as »environmentally sensitive« as possible. The respect for nature included in many Site projects is here reflected in the extensive integration of vegetation.

Das Aqua Center soll so »umweltbewußt« wie möglich sein. Die Achtung vor der Natur, die in vielen Projekten von Site zum Ausdruck kommt, zeigt sich hier in der umfassenden Einbeziehung der Vegetation.

L'Aqua Center se doit d'être aussi soucieux de l'environnement que possible. Le respect de la nature, présent dans de nombreux projets de Site, se reflète ici dans une vaste intégration de la végétation.

ROBERT VENTURI

Robert Venturi (* 1925) may be better known for his 1966 book »Complexity and Contradiction in Architecture« than he is for his built work. Calling on experience gained during a two year stay in Italy, Venturi underlined the importance of Baroque and Mannerist architecture, in contradiction to rectilinear Modernism. His 1972 book, »Learning from Las Vegas« called attention to everyday American architecture and suggested that it could serve as an artistic stimulus. Venturi called for »ugly and ordinary« architecture, as opposed to the »heroism« associated with many 20th century efforts to improve the built environment. With age, and practical experience, Venturi's radical ideas were tempered to the point that even the architecturally conservative Prince Charles could approve of his Sainsbury Wing (National Gallery of Art, London, 1986-91).

Robert Venturi (* 1925) ist vielleicht eher durch sein 1966 erschienenes Buch »Complexity and Contradiction in Architecture« (dt. 1978) bekannt geworden als durch seine Bauten. Er greift darin auf Erfahrungen zurück, die er während eines zweijährigen Aufenthalts in Italien sammelte, und betont die Architektur des Barock und des Manierismus im Gegensatz zur geradlinigen Moderne. Sein Buch »Learning from Las Vegas« (1972, dt. 1979) richtet die Aufmerksamkeit auf die Architektur der amerikanischen Alltagswelt und schlägt vor, diese als künstlerischen Stimulans einzubeziehen. Venturi fordert eine »häßliche und gewöhnliche« Architektur, ganz im Gegensatz zu vielen »heroischen« Versuchen des 20. Jahrhunderts, die bebaute Umgebung zu verschönern. Im Laufe der Zeit sind Venturis radikale Ideen so weit gemäßigt worden, daß heute sogar ein Freund konservativer Architektur wie Prinz Charles den Sainsbury Wing der National Gallery in London (1986-91) gutheißen kann.

Robert Venturi, né en 1925, est sans doute plus connu pour un livre paru en 1966, «Complexity and Contradiction in Architecture» que pour son œuvre construite. S'appuyant sur une expérience acquise pendant un séjour de deux ans en Italie, il y soulignait l'importance de l'architecture baroque et maniériste par opposition à la rigueur rectiligne du Modernisme. Son livre de 1972, «Learning from Las Vegas» attira l'attention sur l'architecture commune américaine et suggéra qu'elle pouvait servir de stimulus artistique. Venturi appela à «une architecture laide et ordinaire», opposée à «l'héroïsme» associé aux efforts du XXème siècle d'améliorer l'environnement construit. Avec l'âge – et l'expérience pratique – les idées radicales de Venturi se tempérèrent à un tel point, que même le Prince Charles, conservateur pour ce qui est de l'architecture, approuva son projet pour la nouvelle aile Sainsbury de la National Gallery of Art (Londres, 1986-91).

The Sainsbury Wing, National Gallery of Art, London, England, 1986–91

Architecture should deal in allusion and symbolism.

Architektur sollte mit Anspielungen und Symbolen arbeiten.

L'architecture devrait prendre en compte l'allusion et le symbolisme.

ROBERT VENTURI

A monumental off-axis stair-case and second floor exhibition galleries, with detailing
in »pietra serena«, give a feeling of solidity
to the building, whose lighting was inspired
by Dulwich.

Die große aus der Achse gerückte Treppe
und die Ausstellungsräume der zweiten Etage mit Detailarbeiten in »pietra serena«
geben dem Gebäude, zusammen mit der
von Dulwich inspirierten Beleuchtung,
einen Ausdruck der Solidität.

Un escalier monumental, mais décalé par
rapport à l'axe du bâtiment, et les salles
d'exposition du second niveau aux finitions
en «pietra serena» confèrent un sentiment
de solidité à ce bâtiment dont l'éclairage a
été inspiré par l'exemple de Dulwich.

GALLERY LEVEL

MEZZANINE LEVEL

STREET LEVEL

BASEMENT MEZZANINE LEVEL

BASEMENT LEVEL

TRANSVERSE SECTION
AN EXTENSION TO THE NATIONAL GALLERY
TRAFALGAR SQUARE · LONDON
VENTURI, RAUCH AND SCOTT BROWN
MARCH, 1987

THE SAINSBURY WING, NATIONAL GALLERY OF ART 1986-91
LONDON, ENGLAND

Due to the circumstances of its construction, and its location, this will remain Robert Venturi's best-known building. Chosen after Prince Charles ridiculed a project by other architects, Venturi made his addition to the National Gallery as unobtrusive as possible. Despite its historically sensitive Trafalgar Square location, it still manages to conserve a certain originality. Its generous top-lit gallery spaces make this building an elegant solution to the requirements of the museum.

Aufgrund seiner Form und Lage wird der Sainsbury-Flügel das bekannteste von Robert Venturis Bauwerken bleiben. Nachdem Prince Charles die Entwürfe anderer Architekten spöttisch abgelehnt hatte, gestaltete Venturi seinen Anbau an die National Gallery so unaufdringlich wie möglich. Dennoch behielt das Objekt auch inmitten seiner historisch exponierten Lage am Trafalgar Square eine gewisse Eigenständigkeit. Die großzügigen, von oben beleuchteten Galerien bilden eine elegante Lösung für die Bedürfnisse des Museums.

Les circonstances de la construction de ce bâtiment et sa localisation en ont fait l'œuvre la plus célèbre de Venturi. Retenu, après que le Prince Charles se soit moqué d'un projet conçu par d'autres architectes, Venturi décida de rendre cette extension de la National Gallery aussi discrète que possible. Dans ce site historique sensible, Trafalgar Square, il a réussi à préserver une certaine originalité. Avec ses galeries à l'éclairage zénithal généreux, cette nouvelle aile apporte une réponse élégante aux besoins du musée.

BIOGRAPHIES

ARQUITECTONICA

Bernardo Fort-Brescia was born in Lima, Peru in 1951. Bachelor of Arts in Architecture and Urban Planning, Princeton University (1973); Master of Architecture, Harvard University (1975). Principal at Arquitectonica since its founding in 1977 in Miami. Laurinda Hope Spear was born in Rochester, Minnesota in 1950. Master of Architecture, Columbia University (1975); Master in City Planning, M. I. T. Principal at Arquitectonica with her husband since its founding. Main buildings: Spear House, Miami, Florida (1976-78); The Palace, Miami, Florida (1979-82); The Atlantis, Miami, Florida (1980-82); Mulder House, Lima, Peru (1983-85); Banco de Crédito, Lima, Peru (1983-88); North Dade Justice Center, Miami, Florida (1984-87); Center for Innovative Technology, Herndon, Virginia (1985-88).

Bernardo Fort-Brescia wurde 1951 in Lima, Peru geboren. Bachelor of Arts in Architektur und Stadtplanung, Princeton University (1973); Master of Architecture, Harvard University (1975). Er leitet Arquitectonica seit 1977. Laurinda Hope Spear wurde 1950 in Rochester, Minnesota geboren. Master of Architecture, Columbia University (1975), Master of City Planning am Massachusetts Institute of Technology. Leitet mit ihrem Mann Arquitectonica seit der Gründung. Wichtige Bauten: Spear House, Miami, Florida (1976-78); The Palace, Miami, Florida (1979-82); The Atlantis, Miami, Florida (1980-82); Mulder House, Lima, Peru (1983-85); Banco de Crédito, Lima, Peru (1983-88); North Dade Justice Center, Miami, Florida (1984-87); Center for Inno-vative Technology, Herndon, Virginia (1985-88).

Bernardo Fort-Brescia est né à Lima, Pérou, en 1951. Diplômé en architecture et urbanisme de Princeton University (1973), Master d'architecture à Harvard University (1975). Principal responsable d'Arquitectonica depuis sa fondation en 1977 à Miami. Laurinda Hope Spear est née à Rochester, Minnesota, en 1950. Master d'architecture de Columbia University (1975), Master d'urbanisme au M. I. T. Responsable d'Arquitectonica depuis sa fondation avec son mari. Principales réalisations: Spear House, Miami, Floride (1976-78); Le Palace, Miami, Floride (1979-82); L'Atlantis, Miami, Floride (1980-82); Mulder House, Lima, Pérou (1983-85); Banco de Crédito, Lima, Pérou (1983-88); North Dade Justice Center, Miami, Floride (1984-87); Center for Innovative Technology, Herndon, Virginie (1985-88).

ARQUITECTONICA, 2151 LeJeune Road, Suite 300, Coral Gables, FL 33134, USA. Fax: 305-445-5865.

PETER EISENMAN

Born in New York in 1932, Bachelor of Architecture, Cornell University, Master of Architecture, Columbia University, Masters and PhD degrees, University of Cambridge. Peter Eisenman has taught at Cambridge, Princeton, Yale and Harvard, as well as the University of Illinois and Ohio State University. Numerous books, including »Moving Arrows, Eros and Other Errors« (Oxford University Press). Main buildings: Wexner Center for the Visual Arts, Ohio State University, Columbus, Ohio (1982-89); Koizumi Sangyo Building, Tokyo, Japan (1987-89); Greater Columbus Convention Center, Columbus, Ohio (1989-93).

Geboren 1932 in New York. Bachelor of Architecture, Cornell University, Master of Architecture, Columbia University, Master und Promotion, University of Cambridge. Peter Eisenman lehrte in Cambridge, Princeton, Yale und Harvard, an der Universität von Illinois und der Ohio State University. Zahlreiche Bücher, darunter »Moving Arrows, Eros and Other Errors« (Oxford University Press). Wichtige Bauten: Wexner Center for the Visual Arts, Ohio State University, Columbus, Ohio (1982-89); Koizumi Sangyo Gebäude, Tokio, Japan (1987-89); Greater Columbus Convention Center, Columbus, Ohio (1989-93).

Né à New York en 1932, diplômé d'Architecture de Cornell University, Master d'architecture de Columbia University, Masters et PhD de l'Université de Cambridge. Peter Eisenman a enseigné à Cambridge, Princeton, Yale, Harvard ainsi qu'à l'Université de l'Illinois et à l'Ohio State University. Auteur de nombreux livres dont «Moving Arrows, Eros and other Errors» (Oxford University Press). Principales réalisations: Wexner Center for the Visual Arts, Ohio State University, Columbus, Ohio (1982-89); Koizumi Sangyo Building, Tokyo, Japon (1987-89); Greater Columbus Convention Center, Ohio, (1989-93).

Eisenman Architects, 40 West 25th Street, New York, NY 10010, USA. Fax 212-645-0726.

FRANK O. GEHRY

Born in Toronto, Canada in 1929. Studied at the University of Southern California, Los Angeles (1949-51), and at Harvard (1956-57). Principal of Frank O. Gehry and Associates, Inc., Los Angeles, since 1962. 1989 Pritzker Prize.
Main buildings: Loyola Law School, Los Angeles, California (1981-84); California Aerospace Museum, Los Angeles, California (1983-84); Norton Residence, Venice, California (1983); Schnabel Residence, Brentwood, California (1989); Festival Disney, Marne-la-Vallée, France (1989-92); University of Toledo Art Building, Toledo, Ohio (1990-92); American Center, Paris, France (1993); Disney Concert Hall, Los Angeles (1989-).

Geboren 1929 in Toronto, Kanada, studierte Frank O. Gehry an der University of Southern California in Los Angeles (1949-51) und in Harvard (1956-57). Seit 1962 leitet er das Büro Frank O. Gehry and Associates, Inc., Los Angeles. Pritzker Preis 1989.
Wichtige Bauten: Loyola Law School, Los Angeles, Kalifornien (1981-84); California Aerospace Museum, Los Angeles, Kalifornien (1983-84); Norton Residence, Venice, Kalifornien (1983); Schnabel Residence, Brentwood, Kalifornien (1989); Festival Disney, Marne-la-Vallée, Frankreich (1989-92); University of Toledo Art Building, Toledo, Ohio (1990-92); American Center, Paris, Frankreich (1993); Disney Concert Hall, Los Angeles, Kalifornien (1989-).

Né à Toronto, Canada en 1929. Études: University of Southern California, Los Angeles (1949-51) et Harvard University (1956-57). Responsable de Frank O. Gehry and Associates, Inc., Los Angeles, Californie, depuis 1962. Pritzker Prize, 1989. Principales réalisations: Loyola Law School, Los Angeles, Californie (1981-84); California Aerospace Museum, Los Angeles, Californie (1983-84); Norton Residence, Venice, Californie (1983); Schnabel Residence, Brentwood, Californie (1989); Festival Disney, Marne-la-Vallée, France (1989-92); University of Toledo Art Building, Toledo, Ohio (1990-92); American Center, Paris, France (1993); Disney Concert Hall, Los Angeles (1989-).

Frank O. Gehry & Associates, Inc., 1520-B Cloverfield Boulevard, Santa Monica, CA 90404, USA. Fax 310-828-2098.

CHARLES GWATHMEY

Born in Charlotte, North Carolina in 1938, Charles Gwathmey studied at the University of Pennsylvania (1956-59), and at Yale University (Master of Architecture, 1962). He founded the firm of Gwathmey, Siegel & Associates in 1968 in New York. Has taught at Princeton, Columbia, the University of Texas, U. C. L. A., and Yale.
Main buildings: American Museum of the Moving Image, Astoria, New York (1988); Fogg Art Museum, Busch-Reisinger/Fine Arts Library Addition, Harvard University, Cambridge, Massachusetts (1990); Disney World Convention Center, Orlando, Florida (1991); Solomon R. Guggenheim Museum, Addition, Renovation and Expansion, New York (1992).

1938 in Charlotte, North Carolina geboren, studierte Charles Gwathmey an der University of Pennsylvania (1956-59) und in Yale (Master of Architecture, 1962). 1968 gründete er das Büro Gwathmey, Siegel & Associates in New York. Er lehrte in Princeton, an der Columbia University, der University of Texas, U. C. L. A. und in Yale.
Wichtige Bauten: American Museum of the Moving Image, Astoria, New York (1988); Anbau des Fogg Art Museum, Busch-Reisinger Fine Arts Library, Harvard University, Cambridge, Massachusetts (1990); Disney World Convention Center, Orlando, Florida (1991); Renovierung und Erweiterung des Solomon R. Guggenheim Museums, New York, New York (1992).

Né à Charlotte, Caroline du Nord, en 1938, Charles Gwathmey a étudié à l'Université de Pennsylvanie (1956-59) et à Yale University (Master d'architecture en 1962) et fondé Gwathmey, Siegel & Associates en 1968 à New York. Il a enseigné à Princeton, Columbia University, University of Texas, U. C. L. A. et Yale.
Principales réalisations: American Museum of the Moving Image, Astoria, New York (1988); Fogg Art Museum, annexe de la Busch-Reisinger/Fine Arts Library, Harvard University, Cambridge, Massachusetts (1990); Disney World Convention Center, Orlando, Floride (1991); annexe, rénovation et extension du Solomon R. Guggenheim Museum, New York, New York (1992).

Gwathmey, Siegel & Associates Architects, 475 Tenth Avenue, New York, NY 10018, USA. Fax 212-967-0890.

STEVEN HOLL

Born in 1947 in Bremerton, Washington. Studied at the University of Washington, in Rome, and at the Architectural Association in London (1976). Began his career in California, and opened his own office in New York (1976). Has taught at the University of Washington, Syracuse University, the Pratt Institute and, since 1981, at Columbia University.
Main buildings: Hybrid Building, Seaside, Florida (1984-88); Berlin AGB Library, Berlin, Germany, competition (1988); Void Space/Hinged Space, Housing, Nexus World, Fukuoka, Japan (1989-91); Stretto House, Dallas, Texas (1989-92).

Geboren 1947 in Bremerton, Washington. Studium an der University of Washington, in Rom und an der Architectural Association in London (1976). Holl begann seine Karriere in Kalifornien und eröffnete 1976 sein eigenes Büro in New York. Er lehrte an der University of Washington, an der Syracuse University, am Pratt Institute und seit 1981 an der Columbia University.
Wichtige Bauten: Hybrid Building, Seaside, Florida (1984-88); Wettbewerb der Berliner AGB Bibliothek, Berlin (1988); Void Space/Hinged Space Wohnhäuser Nexus World, Fukuoka, Japan (1989-91); Stretto House, Dallas, Texas (1989-92).
Né en 1947 à Bremerton, Washington. Etudie à l'Université de Washington, à Rome et à l'Architectural Association à Londres (1976). Commence sa carrière en Californie et ouvre son propre cabinet à New York en 1976. A enseigné à l'Université de Washington, Syracuse University, The Pratt Institute et depuis 1981, à Columbia University.

Principales réalisations: Hybrid Building, Seaside, Floride (1984-88); Bibliothèque AGB, Berlin, Allemagne, concours (1988); Void Space/Hinged Space Housing, Nexus World, Fukuoka, Japon (1989-91); Stretto House, Dallas, Texas (1989-92).

Steven Holl Architects, 435 Hudson Street 4th Fl, New York, NY 10014, USA. Fax 212-463-9718.

HELMUT JAHN

Born in Nuremberg, Germany, 1940. Studied at the Technische Hochschule, Munich (1960-65); and at the Illinois Institute of Technology (1966-67). Entered C. F. Murphy in Chicago in 1967, and became a partner of the firm in 1973. President of Murphy/ Jahn (1982).
Main buildings: Chicago Board of Trade Addition, Chicago, Illinois (1982); Terminal 1 Complex – United Airlines, O'Hare International Airport, Chicago, Illinois (1983-87); One Liberty Place, Philadelphia, Pennsylvania (1984-87); State of Illinois Center, Chicago (1985); Messeturm, Frankfurt, Germany (1985-91).

Geboren 1940 in Nürnberg. Er studierte an der TH in München (1960-65) und am Illinois Institute of Technology (1966-67). 1967 trat er in das Büro von C. F. Murphy ein und wurde 1973 dessen Partner. Seit 1982 leitet er das Büro Murphy/Jahn. Wichtige Bauten: Anbau des Chicago Board of Trade, Chicago, Illinois (1982); Terminal 1 Complex – United Airlines, O'Hare International Airport, Chicago, Illinois (1983-87); One Liberty Place, Philadelphia, Pennsylvania (1984-87); State of

Illinois Center, Chicago, Illinois (1985); Messeturm Frankfurt (1985-91).

Né à Nuremberg, Allemagne, en 1940. Etudes à la Technische Hochschule de Munich (1960-65) et à l'Illinois Institute of Technology (1966-67). Travaille pour C. F. Murphy à Chicago en 1967 avant de devenir partenaire de la firme en 1973, puis Président de Murphy/ Jahn, en 1982.
Principales réalisations: Annexe du Chicago Board of Trade, Chicago, Illinois (1982); Terminal 1 Complex – United Airlines, O'Hare International Airport, Chicago (1983-87); One Liberty Place, Philadelphie, Pennsylvanie (1984-87); State of Illinois Center, Chicago (1985); Tour de la Foire, Francfort-sur-le-Main, Allemagne (1985-91).

Murphy/Jahn, Inc. Architects, 35 East Wacker Drive, Chicago, IL 80801, USA. Fax 312-332-0274.

RICHARD MEIER

Born in Newark, New Jersey in 1934. Richard Meier received his architectural training at Cornell University, and worked in the office of Marcel Breuer (1960-63) before establishing his own practice in 1963. Pritzker Prize, 1984; Royal Gold Medal, 1988.
Main buildings: The Atheneum, New Harmony, Indiana (1975-79); Museum for the Decorative Arts, Frankfurt, Germany (1979-84); High Museum of Art, Atlanta, Georgia (1980-83); Canal Plus Headquarters, Paris, France (1988-91); Getty Center, Los Angeles, California (1984-probably 1996).

170

Geboren 1934 in Newark, New Jersey. Meier erhielt seine Ausbildung an der Cornell University und arbeitete im Büro von Marcel Breuer (1960-63), bevor er 1963 sein eigenes Büro eröffnete. 1984 gewann er den Pritzker Preis, 1988 die Royal Gold Medal.
Wichtige Bauten: The Atheneum, New Harmony, Indiana (1975-79); Museum für Kunsthandwerk, Frankfurt (1979-84); High Museum of Art, Atlanta, Georgia (1980-83); Zentrale des Canal Plus, Paris, Frankreich (1988-91); Getty Center, Los Angeles, Kalifornien (1984–ca. 1996).

Né à Newark, New Jersey, en 1934. Richard Meier a reçu sa formation d'architecte à Cornell University et a travaillé dans le cabinet de Marcel Breuer (1960-63) avant de s'installer à son compte en 1963. Pritzker Prize, 1984; Royal Gold Medal, 1988.
Principales réalisations: The Atheneum, New Harmony, Indiana (1975-79); Musée des Arts décoratifs, Francfort sur le Main, Allemagne (1979-84); High Museum of Art, Atlanta, Georgie (1980-83); Siège social de Canal Plus, Paris, France (1988-91); Getty Center, Los Angeles, Californie (1984-96 probablement).

Richard Meier, 475 Tenth Avenue, New York, NY 10018, USA. Fax 212-967-3207.

CHARLES MOORE

Charles Moore was born in 1925 in Benton Harbor, Michigan. Bachelor of Architecture, University of Michigan, (1947); M. F. A. (1956), PhD (1957), Princeton University. Chairman, Department of Architecture, University of California,
Berkeley (1962-65); Chairman, Department of Architecture, Yale University (1965-69); Dean, School of Architecture and Planning, Yale University (1969-70). His current firm, as of 1991, is Moore/Andersson Architects.
Main buildings: Kresge College, University of California at Santa Cruz (1966-74); Piazza d'Italia, New Orleans, Louisiana (1977-78); Tegel Harbor Housing, Berlin, Germany (1980-87); Church of the Nativity, Rancho Santa Fe, California (1990); Nishiokamoto Housing, Kobe, Japan (1990).

Geboren 1925 in Benton Harbor, Michigan. Bachelor of Architecture, University of Michigan (1947); M. F. A. (1956), PhD (1957), Princeton University. Leiter des Fachbereichs Architektur der University of California, Berkeley (1962-65); Leiter des Fachbereichs Architektur der Yale University (1965-69); Dekan der Fakultät für Architektur und Entwurfsplanung, Yale University (1969-70). 1991 gründete er Moore/Andersson Architects.
Wichtige Bauten: Kresge College, University of California in Santa Cruz (1966-74); Piazza d'Italia, New Orleans, Louisiana (1977-78); Wohnanlage Tegeler Hafen, Berlin (1980-87); Church of the Nativity, Rancho Santa Fe, Kalifornien (1990); Nishiokamoto Wohnanlage, Kobe, Japan (1990).

Charles Moore est né en 1925 à Benton Harbor, Michigan. Diplômé en architecture de l'Université du Michigan en 1947; Master of Fine Arts (1956), PhD (1957), Princeton University. Président du Département d'architecture, University of California, Berkeley (1962-65); Président du Département d'Architecture de Yale University (1965-69); Doyen de l'Ecole d'Architecture et d'Urbanisme, Yale University (1969-70). Depuis 1991, son cabinet s'appelle Moore/Andersson Architects.
Principales réalisations: Kresge College, University of California at Santa Cruz (1966-74); Piazza d'Italia, New Orleans, Louisiane (1977-78); Projet d'habitations pour le port de Tegel, Berlin, Allemagne (1980-87); Eglise de la Nativité, Rancho Santa Fe, Californie (1990); Immeuble d'habitation de Nishiokamoto, Kobe, Japon (1990).

Moore/Andersson Architects, 2102 Quarry Road, Austin, TX 78703, USA. Fax 512-476-0858.

MORPHOSIS

Morphosis' principal Thom Mayne received his Bachelor of Architecture in 1968, and his Master of Architecture at Harvard University in 1978. Has taught at U. C. L. A., Harvard, and Yale.
Main buildings: Lawrence House, California (1981); Cedar's Sinai Comprehensive Cancer Care Center, Beverly Hills, California (1987); Crawford Residence, Montecito, California (1987-92); Los Angeles Arts Park, Performing Arts Pavilion, Los Angeles, California, competition (1989); Yuzen Vintage Car Museum, West Hollywood, California, project (1992).

Der Leiter von Morphosis, Thom Mayne, erhielt 1968 seinen Bachelor of Architecture und 1978 seinen Master of Architecture der Harvard University. Er lehrte an der U. C. L. A., in Harvard und Yale.
Wichtige Bauten: Lawrence House, Kalifornien (1981); Cedar's Sinai Comprehen-

sive Cancer Care Center, Beverly Hills, Kalifornien (1987); Crawford Residence, Montecito, Kalifornien (1987-92); Los Angeles Arts Park, Wettbewerb für den Performing Arts Pavilion, Los Angeles, Kalifornien (1989); Planung für das Yuzen Vintage Car Museum, West Hollywood, Kalifornien (1992).

Le principal responsable de Morphosis, Thom Mayne, a passé son diplôme d'architecte en 1968 et son Master à Harvard University en 1978. Il a enseigné à U. C. L. A., Harvard et Yale.
Principales réalisations: Lawrence House, Californie (1981); Cedar's Sinai Comprehensive Cancer Care Center, Beverly Hills, Californie (1987); Crawford Residence, Montecito, Californie (1987-92); Los Angeles Arts Park, concours pour le Performing Arts Pavilion, Los Angeles, Californie, (1989); Yuzen Vintage Car Museum, West Hollywood, Californie, projet (1992).

MORPHOSIS, 1718 22nd Street, Santa Monica, CA 90404, USA. Fax 310-829-3270.

ERIC OWEN MOSS

Born in Los Angeles, California in 1943, Eric Owen Moss received his Bachelor of Arts degree from U. C. L. A. in 1965, and his Master of Architecture in 1968. He also received a Master's of Architecture degree from Harvard in 1972. Professor of Design at the Southern California Institute of Architecture since 1974. He opened his own firm in 1976.
Main buildings: Central Housing Office, University of California at Irvine, Irvine,

California (1986-89); Lindblade Tower, Culver City, California (1987-89); Paramount Laundry, Culver City, California (1987-89); Gary Group, Culver City, California (1988-90).

Geboren 1943 in Los Angeles, Kalifornien. Moss erhielt 1965 den Bachelor of Arts von der U. C. L. A. und 1968 den Master of Architecture. 1972 erhielt er den Master of Architecture in Harvard. Seit 1974 ist Moss Professor of Design am Southern California Institute of Architecture. 1976 gründete er sein Büro.
Wichtige Bauten: Central Housing Office, University of California at Irvine, Irvine, Kalifornien (1986-89); Lindblade Tower, Culver City, Kalifornien (1987-89); Paramount Laundry, Culver City, Kalifornien (1987-89); Gary Group, Culver City, Kalifornien (1988-90).

Né à Los Angeles, Californie, en 1943, Eric Owen Moss a été diplômé en 1965 et a passé deux Masters en architecture, en 1968 à U. C. L. A. et en 1972, à Harvard University. Il enseigne le design au Southern California Institute of Architecture depuis 1974 et a ouvert son propre cabinet en 1976.
Principales réalisations: Central Housing Office, University of California at Irvine, Irvine, Californie (1986-89); Lindblade Tower, Culver City, Californie (1987-89); Paramount Laundry, Culver City, Californie (1987-89); Gary Group, Culver City, Californie (1988-90).

Eric Owen Moss Architects, 8557 Higuera Street, Culver City, CA 90232, USA. Fax 310-839-7922.

IEOH MING PEI

Born in 1917 in Canton (now Guangzhou), China. Pei came to the United States in 1935. Bachelor of Architecture, M. I. T. (1940), Masters, Harvard University (1942), Doctorat, Harvard University (1946). Formed I. M. Pei & Associates, 1955. AIA Gold Medal, 1979; Pritzker Prize, 1983; Praemium Imperiale, Japan 1989.
Main buildings: National Center for Atmospheric Research, Boulder, Colorado (1961-67); Federal Aviation Agency Air Traffic Control Towers, 50 buildings, various locations (1962-70); John F. Kennedy Library, Boston, Massachusetts (1965-79); National Gallery of Art, East Building, Washington, D. C. (1968-78); Bank of China Tower, Hong Kong (1982-89); Le Grand Louvre, Paris (1983-93).

Pei wurde 1917 in Canton (heute Guangzhou), China geboren und kam 1935 in die USA. 1940 erhielt er den Bachelor of Architecture am M. I. T., 1942 den Master und 1946 den Doktortitel in Harvard. 1955 gründete er I. M. Pei & Associates. 1979 erhielt er die AIA Gold Medal, 1983 den Pritzker Preis, 1989 die japanische Praemium Imperiale Auszeichnung.
Wichtige Bauten: National Center for Atmospheric Research, Boulder, Colorado (1961-67); Federal Aviation Agency Air Traffic Control Towers, 50 Gebäude an verschiedenen Orten (1962-70); John F. Kennedy Library, Boston, Massachusetts (1965-79); National Gallery of Art, Ostflügel, Washington, D. C. (1968-78); Bank of China Tower, Hongkong (1982-89); Le Grand Louvre, Paris (1983-93).

Né en 1917 à Canton, Chine, Pei est arrivé aux Etats-Unis en 1935. Diplôme d'architecture au M. I. T. (1940), Master à Harvard University (1942), Doctorat à Harvard University (1946). Crée I. M. Pei & Associates en 1955. Médaille d'or AIA, 1979; Pritzker Prize, 1983; Prix Impérial du Japon, 1989.
Principales réalisations: National Center for Atmospheric Research, Boulder, Colorado (1961-67); Federal Aviation Agency Air Traffic Control Towers, 50 édifices en différents lieux (1962-70); Bibliothèque John F. Kennedy, Boston, Massachusetts (1965-79); National Gallery of Art, East Building, Washington, D. C., (1968-78); Tour de la Banque de Chine, Hong Kong (1982-89); Projet du Grand Louvre, Paris, France (1983-93).

I. M. Pei Architect, 600 Madison Avenue, New York, NY 10022, USA. Fax 212-872-5443.

ANTOINE PREDOCK

Born in 1936 in Lebanon, Missouri, educated at the University of New Mexico and at Columbia University (Bachelor of Architecture, 1962). Antoine Predock has been the principal of his own firm since 1967. He has taught at U. C. L. A. and California State Polytechnic University.
Main buildings: Nelson Fine Arts Center, Arizona State University, Tempe, Arizona (1986-89); Zuber House, Phoenix, Arizona (1986-89); Hotel Santa Fe, Euro Disney, Marne-la-Vallée, France (1992); Classroom/Laboratory/Administration Building, California Polytechnic University, Pomona, California (1993).

1936 in Lebanon, Arizona geboren, erhielt er seine Ausbildung an der University of New Mexico und der Columbia University (Bachelor of Architecture, 1962). Seit 1967 leitet Antoine Predock ein eigenes Büro. Er lehrte an der U. C. L. A. und an der California State Polytechnic University.
Wichtige Bauten: Nelson Fine Arts Center, Arizona State University, Tempe, Arizona (1986-89); Zuber House, Phoenix, Arizona (1986-89); Hotel Santa Fe, Euro Disney, Marne-la-Vallée, Frankreich (1992); Klassenzimmer, Labor, Verwaltungsbau der California Polytechnic University, Pomona, Kalifornien (1993).

Né en 1936 à Lebanon, Missouri, études à l'Université du Nouveau-Mexique et à Columbia University (Diplômé en architecture en 1962). Antoine Predock dirige son propre cabinet depuis 1967 et a enseigné à U. C. L. A. et à la California State Polytechnic University.
Principales réalisations: Nelson Fine Arts Center, Arizona State University, Tempe, Arizona (1986-89); Zuber House, Phoenix, Arizona (1986-89); Hôtel Santa Fe, Euro Disney, Marne-la-Vallée, France (1992); Classe, laboratoire et bâtiment administratif de la California Polytechnic University, Pomona, Californie (1993).

Antoine Predock Architect, 300 12th Street NW, Albuquerque, NM 87102, USA. Fax 505-243-6254.

BART PRINCE

Born in Albuquerque, New Mexico in 1947. Bachelor of Architecture, Arizona State University (1970). Worked with

Bruce Goff from 1968 to 1973, assisted him in the design of the Pavilion for Japanese Art, Los Angeles County Museum of Art, Los Angeles, California (1978-89), and completed the building after Goff's death in 1982. Opened his architectural practice in 1973.
Main buildings: Bart Prince Residence and studio, Albuquerque, New Mexico (1983); Joe Price Residence, Corona del Mar, California (1986); Brad and June Prince House, Albuquerque, New Mexico (1988); Nolan Residence, Taos, New Mexico (1993).

Geboren 1947 in Albuquerque, New Mexico. 1970 erhielt er den Bachelor of Architecture der Arizona State University. Von 1968 bis 1973 arbeitete er mit Bruce Goff zusammen, assistierte ihm beim Entwurf des Pavillons für japanische Kunst des Los Angeles County Museum of Art, Los Angeles, Kalifornien (1978-89) und stellte das Gebäude nach Goffs Tod 1982 fertig. Eigenes Büro seit 1973.
Wichtige Bauten: Bart Prince Residence und Studio, Albuquerque, New Mexico (1983); Joe Price Residence, Corona del Mar, Kalifornien (1986); Brad and June Prince House, Albuquerque, New Mexico (1988); Nolan Residence, Taos, New Mexico (1993).

Né à Albuquerque, Nouveau-Mexique, en 1947. Diplômé d'architecture de l'Arizona State University (1947). Travaille avec Bruce Goff de 1968 à 1973 et l'assiste pour la création du Pavillon de l'Art Japonais, Los Angeles County Museum of Art, Los Angeles, Californie (1978-89), et complétera le bâtiment à la mort de Goff en 1982. Ouvre son propre cabinet en 1973.

Principales réalisations: Bart Prince Residence et Studio à Albuquerque, Nouveau-Mexique (1983); Joe Price Residence, Corona del Mar, Californie (1986); Brad and June Prince House, Albuquerque, Nouveau-Mexique (1988); Nolan Residence, Taos, Nouveau-Mexique (1993).

Bart Prince Architect, 3501 Monte Vista NE, Albuquerque, NM 87106, USA. Fax 505-268-9045.

SITE

James Wines, founding principal of Site (Sculpture in the Environment) was born in Chicago, Illinois, and studied at Syracuse University art and art history. Between 1955 and 1968, he was a sculptor. Alison Sky, also a founding principal was born in New York and received a degree in fine arts from Adelphi University. Main buildings: Indeterminate Façade Showroom, Houston, Texas (1975); Ghost Parking Lot, Hamden, Connecticut (1978); Forest Building, Henrico, Virginia (1980); Highway 86, World Exposition, Vancouver, British Columbia, Canada (1986); Four Continents Bridge, Hiroshima, Japan (1989); Avenue 5, Universal Exhibition, Seville, Spain (1992).

James Wines, Gründer von Site (Sculpture in the Environment), ist in Chicago, Illinois geboren und studierte an der Syracuse University Kunst und Kunstgeschichte. 1955-68 arbeitete er als Bildhauer. Alison Sky, auch Gründungsmitglied, ist in New York geboren und studierte Kunst an der Adelphi University. Wichtige Bauten: Indeterminate Façade Showroom, Houston, Texas (1975); Ghost

Parking Lot, Hamden, Connecticut (1978); Forest Building, Henrico, Virginia (1980); Highway 86, World Exposition, Vancouver, British Columbia, Kanada (1986); Four Continents Bridge, Hiroshima, Japan (1989); Avenue 5, Sevilla (1992).

James Wines, fondateur et responsable de Site est né à Chicago et a fait ses études à l'Université de Syracuse dont il est diplômé en art et histoire de l'art. Il se consacre à la sculpture de 1955 à 1968. Alison Sky, également fondatrice de Site est née à New York. Diplômé des Beaux-Arts d'Adelphi University.
Principales réalisations: Indeterminate Façade Showroom, Houston, Texas (1975); Ghost Parking Lot, Hamden, Connecticut (1978); Forest Building, Henrico, Virginie (1980); Highway 86, World Exposition, Vancouver, Colombie Britannique, Canada (1986); Pont des Quatre Continents, Hiroshima, Japon, (1989); Avenue 5, Expo'92, Seville, Espagne (1992).

SITE, 65 Bleecker Street, New York, NY 10012, USA. Fax 212-353-3086.

ROBERT VENTURI

Born in Philadelphia in 1925, Robert Venturi studied architecture at Princeton University. Between 1950 and 1958, he worked with O. Stonorov, Eero Saarinen and Louis Kahn. He has taught at Yale and the University of Pennsylvania.
Main buildings: Guild House, Philadelphia, Pennsylvania (1961-64); Franklin Court, Philadelphia, Pennsylvania (1972-76); Brant-Johnson House, Vail, Colorado (1975-77); Gordon Wu Hall, Butler College, Princeton University, Princeton,

New Jersey (1980-83); Seattle Art Museum, Seattle, Washington (1984-91); Sainsbury Wing, National Gallery of Art, London, England (1986-91).

1925 in Philadelphia geboren, studierte Robert Venturi an der Princeton University. Zwischen 1950 und 1958 arbeitete er mit O. Stonorov, Eero Saarinen und Louis Kahn zusammen. Er lehrte in Yale und an der University of Pennsylvania. Wichtige Bauten: Guild House, Philadelphia, Pennsylvania (1961-64); Franklin Court, Philadelphia, Pennsylvania (1972-76); Brant-Johnson House, Vail, Colorado (1975-77); Gordon Wu Hall, Butler College, Princeton University, Princeton, New Jersey (1980-83); Seattle Art Museum, Seattle, Washington (1984-91); Sainsbury Wing, National Gallery of Art, London, England (1986-91).

Né à Philadelphie en 1925, Robert Venturi a étudié l'architecture à Princeton University. De 1950 à 1958, il travaille avec O. Stonorov, Eero Saarinen et Louis Kahn. Il a enseigné à Yale et à l'Université de Pennsylvanie.
Principales réalisations: Guild House, Philadelphie, Pennsylvanie (1961-64); Franklin Court, Philadelphie, Pennsylvanie (1972-76); Brant-Johnson House, Vail, Colorado (1975-77); Gordon Wu Hall, Butler College, Princeton University, Princeton, New Jersey (1980-83); Seattle Art Museum, Seattle, Washington (1984-91); Sainsbury Wing, National Gallery of Art, Londres, Angleterre (1986-91).

Venturi, Scott Brown & Associates, Inc., 4236 Main Street, Philadelphia, PA 19127, USA. Fax 215-487-2520.

INDEX

Illustrations are denoted by page numbers in bold typeface

CREDITS

The publisher and editor wish to thank each of the architects and photographers for their kind assistance.

p. 2 © Photo: Timothy Hursley, Little Rock (AR)
p. 6 © Photo: Paul Warchol, New York
p. 8 © Photo: Esto Photographics, Ezra Stoller
p. 10 © Photo: Esto Photographics, Peter Aaron
p. 12-13 © Photo: Esto Photographics, Jeff Goldberg
p. 14-15 © Photo: Esto Photographics, Ezra Stoller
p. 16 © Photo: Browning/The New York Historical Society
p. 17 © Photo: Esto Photographics, Scott Frances
p. 19 © Photo: Timothy Hursley, Little Rock (AR)
p. 20 © Photo: Esto Photographics, Wayne Andrews
p. 23 © Frank Lloyd Wright Foundation, Scottsdale, Arizona
p. 24-25 © Photo: Christopher Little, New York
p. 26 © Photo: Esto Photographics, Ezra Stoller
p. 27 © Photo: Esto Photographics, Peter Mauss
p. 28 © Photo: Esto Photographics, Jeff Goldberg
p. 30-31 © Photo: Esto Photographics, Ezra Stoller
p. 32-33 above © Photo: Arcaid, Richard Bryant
p. 33 below © Photo: Arcaid, Niall Clutton
p. 34-37 © Photo: Esto Photographics, Peter Aaron
p. 38 © Photo: Norman McGrath, New York
p. 39 © Photo: Timothy Hursley, Little Rock (AR)
p. 40-41 © Site, New York
p. 42 © Photo: Joshua White
p. 43 © Photo: Jochen Littkemann
p. 45 © Moore/Andersson Architects, Austin (TX)
p. 48 © Arquitectonica, Coral Gables (FL)
p. 49 © Photo: Norman McGrath
p. 50-55 © Photo: Timothy Hursley, Little Rock (AR)
p. 57-61 © Photo: Esto Photographics, Jeff Goldberg
p. 62 © Frank O. Gehry & Ass. Inc., Santa Monica (CA)
p. 63 © Photo: Timothy Hursley, Little Rock (AR)
p. 64-65 © Photo: Grant Mudford, Los Angeles
p. 66-69 © Photo: Timothy Hursley, Little Rock (AR)
p. 70-71 © Photo: Karin Heßmann, Dortmund
p. 72-73 © Photo: A. Wolf, Paris
p. 74 © Gwathmey Siegel & Ass. Architects, New York
p. 75-78 © Photo: Esto Photographics, Jeff Goldberg
p. 79-81 © Gwathmey Siegel & Ass. Architects, New York
p. 82 © Steven Holl Architects, New York
p. 83-85 © Photo: Paul Warchol, New York
p. 86-89 © Steven Holl Architects, New York

p. 90-91 © Murphy/Jahn Inc. Architects, Chicago (IL)
p. 92 © Photo: Dieter Leistner, Mainz
p. 94 © Photo: Timothy Hursley, Little Rock (AR)
p. 95-97 © Murphy/Jahn Inc. Architect, Chicago (IL)
p. 98 © Photo: Luca Vignelli
p. 99 © Photo: Esto Photographics, Scott Frances
p. 100 above © Photo: Esto Photographics, Ezra Stoller
p. 100 below © Photo: Esto Photographics, Scott Frances
p. 101 above © Photo: Esto Photographics, Ezra Stoller
p. 101 below © Photo: Dieter Leistner, Mainz
p. 102-103 © Photo: Esto Photographics, Scott Frances
p. 104-105 © J. Paul Getty Trust and Richard Meier & Partners, © Photo: Tom Bonner
p. 106 © Photo: Arcaid, Ezra Stoller
p. 107 © Photo: Esto Photographics, Ezra Stoller
p. 108 © Moore/Andersson Architects, Austin (TX)
p. 109-115 © Photo: Timothy Hursley, Little Rock (AR)
p. 116 © Morphosis, Santa Monica (CA)
p. 117 © Photo: Tom Bonner, Venice (CA)
p. 118-119 © Morphosis, Santa Monica (CA)
p. 120-121 © Photo: Tom Bonner, Venice (CA)
p. 122 © Eric Owen Moss Architects, Culver City (CA)
p. 123-128 above © Photo: Tom Bonner, Venice (CA)
p. 128 below © Photo: Peter Cook
p. 129 © Photo: Tom Bonner, Venice (CA)
p. 130 © Photo: Serge Hambourg
p. 131 © Photo: Paul Warchol, New York
p. 132 © Photo: A. Wolf, Paris
p. 133 © Photo: S. Couturier
p. 134-135 above © Photo: A. Wolf, Paris
p. 135 below © Pei Cobb Freed & Partners Architects, New York
p. 136-137 © Photo: Paul Warchol, New York
p. 138-139 © Photo: Timothy Hursley, Little Rock (AR)
p. 140 © Pei Cobb Freed & Partners Architects, New York
p. 141 © Photo: Arnaud Carpentier
p. 142 © Photo: Robert Reck
p. 143 © Photo: Esto Photographics, Peter Aaron
p. 144-147 © Photo: Timothy Hursley, Little Rock (AR)
p. 149-151 © Photo: Timothy Hursley, Little Rock (AR)
p. 152 © Bart Prince Architect, Albuquerque (NM)
p. 153-155 © Photo: Esto Photographics, Scott Frances
p. 156-163 © Site, New York
p. 164 © Photo: John T. Miller
p. 165-167 © Photo: Matt Wargo Photography, Philadelphia